Sex in the Texts

Paul Yedwab

Sex in the Texts

Paul Yedwab

Katherine Schwartz, Project Editor

URJ Press
New York, New York

Grateful acknowledgement is made to the following publishers for permission to reprint material under copyright:

CCAR Press: For permission to reprint material from *Teshuvot for the Nineties: Reform Judaism's Answers for Today's Dilemmas*, ed. W. Gunther Plaut and Mark Washofsky (New York: CCAR, 1999); and from the "Resolution on Same Gender Officiation," 2000.

The Rabbinical Assembly: For permission to reprint material from "'This Is My Beloved, This is My Friend': A Rabbinic Letter on Intimate Relations," by Elliot N. Dorff (New York: Rabbinical Assembly, 1996).

Library of Congress Cataloging-in-Publication Data
Yedwab, Paul Michael.
    Sex in the texts / Paul Yedwab; Katherine Schwartz, project editor.
    p. cm.
    ISBN 0-8074-0763-1 (pbk.: alk. paper)
    1. Sex—Religious aspects—Judaism. 2. Sex in the Bible.
3. Rabbinical literature. 4. Sex in rabbinical literature. 5. Jewish religious education—Textbooks for teenagers. 6. Jewish religious education—Textbooks for adults. I. Schwartz, Katherine. II. Title.

BM720.S4 Y43 2001
296.3'66–dc21
                                                              2001025701

Typesetting: El Ot Ltd.
This book is printed on acid-free paper
Copyright © 2001 by URJ Press
Manufactured in the United States of America
10 9 8 7 6 5 4 3

Dedication

לא איש בלא אשה ולא אשה בלא איש
ולא שניהם בלא שכינה.

"No man without woman; no woman without man,
and neither without God."

For Wendy, whom I love.

Contents

Acknowledgments

To my colleagues, Rabbi Harold Loss, Rabbi Joshua Bennett, Rabbi Marla Hornsten, Rabbi M. Robert Syme, Cantor Harold Orbach, and Cantor Lori Corrsin, my closest advisors and friends...

To Rabbi Hara Person, my dream editor, whose powerful suggestions are made ever so gently...

To the staff of the UAHC Press, Ken Gesser, Stuart Benick, Rick Abrams, Katherine Schwartz, Liane Broido, and Debra Hirsch Corman, all of whom have lent their expertise to this project...

To Fran Pearlman, our Temple's distinguished educational director, whose idea it was to commit my "Sex in the Texts" curriculum to paper . . .

To Susie Borin, my administrative assistant, who keeps my rabbinic life sane...

To my parents Myra and Rabbi Stanley Yedwab who are my life-long teachers . . .

To Jennifer Tisdale, my research assistant on this project, whose rabbinic future shines so very brightly...

And most of all, to my wife, Wendy, and my children, Ariella, Jesse, and Zoe, who lovingly allowed me to steal time from them in order to complete this book...

THANK YOU. This work would have been ever so much poorer but for your love, your friendship, and your assistance.

Introduction

Mr. Johnson was my seventh-grade gym teacher. He was a big, burly, mountain of a man, who seemed to derive preternatural pleasure from the assigning of push-ups and jumping jacks. We liked him though, for in his own gruff way, Mr. Johnson left no doubt that his primary goal was to model for us "men" the appropriate male characteristics of strength, toughness, and good sportsmanship. When the state board of education mandated that all junior high school students receive one semester of "sex education," Mr. Johnson discovered that the task of teaching that particular "health class" would fall squarely upon his substantial shoulders. I remember vividly the look of pained discomfort on his face as he turned the page in the prepared text only to realize that this was the day he would have to cover masturbation. Menstruation was no easier. Mr. Johnson would have given anything to be back in the gym where he belonged, throwing medicine balls and barking out orders. Given the choice, we would have preferred to endure 300 sit-ups. You can therefore imagine his relief when the "sex education" unit ended and he was free to teach driver's ed at the high school. He may have been putting his life in danger, but at least he did not have to say the word "uterus" in front of thirty adolescent boys.

This experience has shaped my approach to the writing of *Sex in the Texts*. This book is not a Jewish sex manual. It is less "everything you ever wanted to know about sex" and more "what does the Jewish tradition say about sex?" It is intended to evoke comfortable conversation among both adults and teenagers. Our focus, therefore, will be on the texts themselves. What do the Torah, the Bible, the midrash, the Talmud, the commentaries, and the responsa literature have to say about sexual issues? What can we learn from them? Instead of striving only for twenty-first-century relevance, we will try to look directly into the minds of our forebears.

This approach arises out of my belief that, as educators, we too often teach *about* Judaism, rather than teaching Judaism itself. Textbooks supplant primary sources in our homes and in our classrooms. In *Sex in the Texts*, the emphasis will be squarely on the texts.

This does, however, pose a thorny problem. Ancient Jewish texts are often brilliantly insightful and remarkably sensitive to both men's and women's concerns. They also can be sexist, politically incorrect, and even downright wrong. Thus, the editorial voice will not be entirely absent. I am a modern, liberal rabbi. Some of those sensitivities will show through in my choice of texts, in the way that I juxtapose them, and in the conclusions that I draw from them. Nonetheless, because of its emphasis on primary sources, this book should be appropriate for use in the high-school, junior-high, or youth-group programs of synagogues, as part of a day-school curriculum, or as the basis for adult learning. It will also be accessible to the individual learner.

If you come to this book hoping to discover the definitive Jewish opinion on some aspect of human sexuality, I fear you may find yourself frustrated. As you will most surely see, Judaism, in its four-thousand-year history, has had an astonishing breadth of perspectives on every aspect of our sexual lives.

You will also notice that I have defined "sex" very broadly. Sexuality, in my eyes, includes romance, marriage, divorce, dating, gender identity, and sexual politics.

You should also be aware at the outset that our study will not be exhaustive. A comprehensive work on Jewish sexuality would fill many bookshelves. I think you will find, though, that this book is a fine introduction to the study of sacred texts in general and to the exploration of sexuality in Jewish thought in particular.

Before the study of Torah, Jewish texts in all of their various facets, we say a blessing thanking God for giving us the privilege of learning together.

בָּרוּךְ אַתָּה, יְיָ אֱלֹהֵינוּ, מֶלֶךְ הָעוֹלָם, אֲשֶׁר קִדְּשָׁנוּ בְּמִצְוֹתָיו וְצִוָּנוּ
לַעֲסוֹק בְּדִבְרֵי תוֹרָה.

Baruch atah Adonai, Eloheinu Melech haolam, asher kid'shanu b'mitzvotav v'tzivanu laasok b'divrei Torah.

We praise You, Eternal God, Sovereign of the universe: You hallow us with the gift of Torah and command us to immerse ourselves in its words.

Now, let us begin!

1. In the Beginning

Like all good things, sex began in the beginning. Let us begin there as well.

Torah

> The Torah is the cornerstone of the Jewish faith. It is the sacred diary of God's relationship with the People of Israel. The Torah is the first section of the Hebrew Bible and is comprised of the Five Books of Moses: *B'reishit* (Genesis), *Sh'mot* (Exodus), *Vayikra* (Leviticus), *B'midbar* (Numbers), and *D'varim* (Deuteronomy).

Genesis 1:26–28

כו וַיֹּאמֶר אֱלֹהִים נַעֲשֶׂה אָדָם בְּצַלְמֵנוּ כִּדְמוּתֵנוּ וְיִרְדּוּ בִדְגַת הַיָּם וּבְעוֹף הַשָּׁמַיִם וּבַבְּהֵמָה וּבְכָל־הָאָרֶץ וּבְכָל־הָרֶמֶשׂ הָרֹמֵשׂ עַל־הָאָרֶץ:

1:26. And God said, "Let us make man in our image, after our likeness. They shall rule the fish of the sea, the birds of the sky, the cattle, the whole earth, and every creeping creature that crawls on the earth."

כז וַיִּבְרָא אֱלֹהִים אֶת־הָאָדָם בְּצַלְמוֹ בְּצֶלֶם אֱלֹהִים בָּרָא אֹתוֹ זָכָר וּנְקֵבָה בָּרָא אֹתָם:

27. So God created man in God's own image, in the image of God, God created him; male and female God created them.

1

28 וַיְבָרֶךְ אֹתָם אֱלֹהִים וַיֹּאמֶר לָהֶם אֱלֹהִים פְּרוּ וּרְבוּ וּמִלְאוּ
אֶת־הָאָרֶץ וְכִבְשֻׁהָ וּרְדוּ בִּדְגַת הַיָּם וּבְעוֹף הַשָּׁמַיִם וּבְכָל־חַיָּה
הָרֹמֶשֶׂת עַל־הָאָרֶץ:

28. God blessed them and said to them, "Be fruitful and
multiply, fill the earth and master it; and rule over the fish
of the sea, and the birds of the sky, and every living thing
that moves on the earth."

Here we find the first commandment in the Torah: "Be fruitful and
multiply." According to Jewish tradition, 613 commandments are
contained within the Torah text. Is it not remarkable that reproduction
is the very first one? Our very first Jewish obligation, therefore, is built
upon our sexuality. This first commandment, however, leads to many
others. Sexuality carries with it a great deal of responsibility.

*What responsibilities fall upon you once you have put yourself in the
position of "being fruitful and multiplying"? What obligations arise out
of the very first commandment?*

But wait a minute! Isn't something missing here? What happened to
the familiar story of Eve being created from Adam's rib? In this passage,
it seems that God creates man and woman simultaneously: "male and
female God created them." If we read on in the Torah, however, we
find the story we were expecting in the very next chapter.

Genesis 2:18

18 וַיֹּאמֶר יְהוָה אֱלֹהִים לֹא־טוֹב הֱיוֹת הָאָדָם לְבַדּוֹ אֶעֱשֶׂה־לּוֹ
עֵזֶר כְּנֶגְדּוֹ:

2:18. *Adonai* God said, "It is not good for man to be alone;
I will make him a partner to help and complement him."

2

This is a very important line. Why is it "not good for man to be alone"? What does this tell us about human nature?

There is also a very difficult translation problem here. In the Hebrew, God says: "I will make him an עֵזֶר כְּנֶגְדּוֹ *(eizer k'negdo)*. עֵזֶר *(eizer)* means "help," and כְּנֶגְדּוֹ *(k'negdo)* means "as against him." So literally translated, this phrase means "a help as against him."

How could a wife be an עֵזֶר כְּנֶגְדּוֹ (eizer k'negdo), "a help as against" her husband (or vice versa)?

I have translated עֵזֶר כְּנֶגְדּוֹ (eizer k'negdo), as "a partner to help and complement him." It is more commonly translated as "helpmate." How would you have translated this phrase?

But let us return now to our original problem. Where is that story about the rib, anyway? Oh, here it is!

Genesis 2:19–23

19 וַיִּצֶר יְהֹוָה אֱלֹהִים מִן־הָאֲדָמָה כָּל־חַיַּת הַשָּׂדֶה וְאֵת כָּל־עוֹף הַשָּׁמַיִם וַיָּבֵא אֶל־הָאָדָם לִרְאוֹת מַה־יִּקְרָא־לוֹ וְכֹל אֲשֶׁר יִקְרָא־לוֹ הָאָדָם נֶפֶשׁ חַיָּה הוּא שְׁמוֹ:

2:19. And *Adonai* God formed from the earth every beast of the field and every bird of the sky, and brought them to the man to see what he would call them, and whatever the man called each living creature, that became its name.

20 וַיִּקְרָא הָאָדָם שֵׁמוֹת לְכָל־הַבְּהֵמָה וּלְעוֹף הַשָּׁמַיִם וּלְכֹל חַיַּת הַשָּׂדֶה וּלְאָדָם לֹא־מָצָא עֵזֶר כְּנֶגְדּוֹ:

20. And the man assigned names to all the cattle and to the birds of the sky and to every beast of the field, but for Adam, God did not find a fitting partner.

21 וַיַּפֵּל יְהוָה אֱלֹהִים תַּרְדֵּמָה עַל־הָאָדָם וַיִּישָׁן וַיִּקַּח אַחַת
מִצַּלְעֹתָיו וַיִּסְגֹּר בָּשָׂר תַּחְתֶּנָּה:

21. So *Adonai* God caused a deep sleep to fall upon the
man, and he slept, and God took one of his ribs and
closed up the flesh around the wound.

22 וַיִּבֶן יְהוָה אֱלֹהִים אֶת־הַצֵּלָע אֲשֶׁר־לָקַח מִן־הָאָדָם לְאִשָּׁה
וַיְבִאֶהָ אֶל־הָאָדָם:

22. And *Adonai* God fashioned the rib that God had taken
from the man into a woman, and God brought her to the
man.

23 וַיֹּאמֶר הָאָדָם
זֹאת הַפַּעַם
עֶצֶם מֵעֲצָמַי
וּבָשָׂר מִבְּשָׂרִי
לְזֹאת יִקָּרֵא אִשָּׁה
כִּי מֵאִישׁ לֻקֳחָה־זֹּאת:

23. The man said, "This time she is bone of my bones and
flesh of my flesh. This one shall be called woman, for from
man was she taken."

How can we reconcile the two different stories of the creation of
woman? Modern biblical scholars explain this duplication as a weaving
together of two distinct ancient textual traditions by a clever editor, or
"redactor." This approach is known as the Documentary Hypothesis.

If one believes, however, that every word of the Torah was given by
God, then every word must be perfect, and absolutely true, and there
for a reason. This traditional approach does not accept that the Torah
might have been edited by humans, who could have overlooked
contradictions or superfluous words or stories. This approach also

not lie on the bottom during sex," and he said, "I will not lie beneath you. I want to be on top. After all, you are fit only to be in the bottom position, while I am meant to be in the superior one." Lilith answered, "We are equal to each other! Were we not both created from the earth?" Alas, they would not listen to one another. When Lilith saw this, she pronounced God's Ineffable Name and flew away. Adam stood in prayer before his Creator. "Sovereign of the universe," he cried, "the woman you have given me has run away." At once, the Holy One, blessed be, sent three angels to bring her back.

God said to Adam, "If she agrees to come back, so be it. However, if she does not return, she must permit 100 of her children to die every day."

The angels left God's presence, chased after Lilith, and overtook her in the midst of the Red Sea, the very same sea in which the Egyptians were destined to drown. They reported God's words to her, but she did not agree to return, so the angels said, "Then we must drown you in the sea."

"Be off!" she said. "I was created to cause sickness in infants. If the infant is male, I have dominion over him for eight days after his birth, and if female, for twenty days."

When the angels heard Lilith's words, they begged her to go back with them, but she made a compromise with them and sealed it by the name of God. "From now on, whenever I see you, or your names, or your forms in an amulet" she said, "I will have no power over that infant." She also agreed to have 100 of her own children die every day. As a result, 100 demon children perish every day, and for the same reason, we write the angels' names on the amulets of young children. When Lilith sees their names, she remembers her oath, and the child recovers.

Although the *Alphabet of Ben Sira* is not an authoritative Jewish text, this midrash became widely known. Throughout the centuries, Lilith was feared by Jews as a shadowy demon who stole children out of their cribs.

What was the nature of Lilith's "crime"? For what was she punished?

What does this say about the traditional view of women? How does this idea compare or contrast with our modern ideal of the relationship between men and women?

In 1976 a new magazine was born. It was to be a vehicle of expression for the Jewish feminist movement. The editors chose to call their fledgling magazine Lilith. *Why do you think they chose this name?*

2. Sometimes a Snake Is Just a Snake...?

Let us compare two other passages from Genesis and see if we can find the קְשִׁי (koshi).

Genesis 2:15–17

15 וַיִּקַּח יְהוָה אֱלֹהִים אֶת־הָאָדָם וַיַּנִּחֵהוּ בְגַן־עֵדֶן לְעָבְדָהּ וּלְשָׁמְרָהּ:

2:15. *Adonai* God took the man and placed him in the Garden of Eden, to work it and to tend it.

16 וַיְצַו יְהוָה אֱלֹהִים עַל־הָאָדָם לֵאמֹר מִכֹּל עֵץ־הַגָּן אָכֹל תֹּאכֵל:

16. And *Adonai* commanded the man, saying, "Of every tree of the garden you may freely eat;

17 וּמֵעֵץ הַדַּעַת טוֹב וָרָע לֹא תֹאכַל מִמֶּנּוּ כִּי בְּיוֹם אֲכָלְךָ מִמֶּנּוּ מוֹת תָּמוּת:

17. But of the Tree of Knowledge of Good and Evil, you must not eat, for on the day you partake of it, you will surely die."

Now examine the text below for discrepancies in Eve's testimony as to what God said not to do.

9

Genesis 2:25–3:3

כה וַיִּהְיוּ שְׁנֵיהֶם עֲרוּמִּים הָאָדָם וְאִשְׁתּוֹ וְלֹא יִתְבֹּשָׁשׁוּ:

2:25. The two of them were naked, the man and his wife, but they were not ashamed.

א וְהַנָּחָשׁ הָיָה עָרוּם מִכֹּל חַיַּת הַשָּׂדֶה אֲשֶׁר עָשָׂה יְהוָה אֱלֹהִים וַיֹּאמֶר אֶל־הָאִשָּׁה אַף כִּי־אָמַר אֱלֹהִים לֹא תֹאכְלוּ מִכֹּל עֵץ הַגָּן:

3:1. Now the serpent was the most cunning of all the beasts of the field that *Adonai* God had made. He said to the woman, "Did God truly say, 'You shall not eat from any tree of the garden?'"

ב וַתֹּאמֶר הָאִשָּׁה אֶל־הַנָּחָשׁ מִפְּרִי עֵץ־הַגָּן נֹאכֵל:

2. The woman responded to the serpent, "We may eat of the fruit of the trees of the garden,

ג וּמִפְּרִי הָעֵץ אֲשֶׁר בְּתוֹךְ־הַגָּן אָמַר אֱלֹהִים לֹא תֹאכְלוּ מִמֶּנּוּ וְלֹא תִגְּעוּ בּוֹ פֶּן־תְּמֻתוּן:

3. But of the fruit of the tree in the middle of the garden God has said, 'You shall neither eat of it nor touch it, or you will die!'"

What did Eve report that God had said not to do?

What did God actually say not to do?

Why do you suppose that Eve added onto God's words?

Have you ever exaggerated for similar purposes in your own life? When? Why?

The Rabbis could not let such a discrepancy go without comment. In the following midrash, building a "fence around the Torah" refers to the traditional practice of adding restrictions onto the biblical restrictions in order to protect against inadvertent transgression. For instance, the Torah commands us to observe the Sabbath day and keep it holy. Generally a day is twenty-four hours. Tradition, however, added a twenty-fifth hour in order to prevent people from unwittingly violating the Sabbath restrictions. The extra hour is a fence that is placed around the original commandment.

B'reishit Rabbah 19:3

ומפרי העץ אשר בתוך הגן וגו' ולא תגעו בו הה"ד (משלי ל)
אל תוסף על דבריו פן יוכיח בך ונכזבת תני ר' חייא שלא
תעשה את הגדר יותר מן העיקר שלא יפול ויקצץ הנטיעות
כך אמר הקב"ה כי ביום אכלך ממנו וגו' והיא לא אמרה כן
אלא אמר אלהים לא תאכלו ממנו ולא תגעו בו כיון שראה
אותו עוברת לפני העץ נטלה ודחפה עליו אמר לה הא לא
מיתת כמה דלא מיתת במקרביה כן לא מיתת במיכליה.

"BUT OF THE FRUIT OF THE TREE IN THE MIDDLE OF THE GARDEN, GOD HAS SAID, 'YOU SHALL NEITHER EAT OF IT NOR TOUCH IT, OR YOU WILL DIE!'" (Genesis 3:3). Thus it is written, "DO NOT ADD ONTO GOD'S WORDS, OR GOD WILL PUNISH YOU, AS YOU WILL BE A LIAR" (Proverbs 30:6). Rabbi Chiyya taught: That means that you must not make the fence more than the principal thing, lest it fall and destroy the plants. Thus, the Holy One, blessed be, has said, "BUT OF THE TREE OF KNOWLEDGE OF GOOD AND EVIL, YOU MUST NOT EAT, FOR ON THE DAY YOU PARTAKE OF IT, YOU WILL SURELY DIE" (Genesis 2:17). Eve did not say this, but rather, "YOU SHALL NEITHER EAT OF IT NOR TOUCH IT" (Genesis 3:3). When the serpent saw her exaggerating in this manner, he grabbed her and pushed her against the tree. "So, have you died?" he asked her. "Just as you were not stricken when you touched it, so will you not die when you eat from it."

This midrash teaches an interesting lesson. We are not to add onto God's laws, for in doing so we may actually be led to distort them. In other words, we are not to follow the practice of building a fence around the Torah.

Can you think of another example of building a fence around the Torah?

There is clearly a disagreement here. Some would favor protecting the Torah with additional commandments. Our text seems to stand opposed to this practice.

How do you feel about this process of protecting God's commandments with additional restrictions? What are the advantages? What are the disadvantages?

There is, however, another קֹשִׁי (koshi) here that is even more basic. Why would God not want Adam and Eve to eat from the fruit of the Tree of Knowledge of Good and Evil? Is knowledge not a thoroughly positive attribute? Is it not a quality for which we should all strive? In order to answer this question for yourself, it may be helpful to consider the following:

Can there be anything good about being sheltered from knowledge?

Are children in our world today too sheltered or not sheltered enough from knowledge of sexual issues?

The following text may help you with the answer to the last question.

Genesis 3:4–7

4 וַיֹּאמֶר הַנָּחָשׁ אֶל־הָאִשָּׁה לֹא־מוֹת תְּמֻתוּן:

3:4. And the serpent said to the woman, "You will not surely die,

5 כִּי יֹדֵעַ אֱלֹהִים כִּי בְּיוֹם אֲכָלְכֶם מִמֶּנּוּ וְנִפְקְחוּ עֵינֵיכֶם וִהְיִיתֶם כֵּאלֹהִים יֹדְעֵי טוֹב וָרָע:

5. For God knows that on the day you eat of it your eyes will be opened and you will be like God, beings who know good and evil."

6 וַתֵּרֶא הָאִשָּׁה כִּי טוֹב הָעֵץ לְמַאֲכָל וְכִי תַאֲוָה־הוּא לָעֵינַיִם וְנֶחְמָד הָעֵץ לְהַשְׂכִּיל וַתִּקַּח מִפִּרְיוֹ וַתֹּאכַל וַתִּתֵּן גַּם־לְאִישָׁהּ עִמָּהּ וַיֹּאכַל:

6. When the woman saw that the tree was good for eating and delightful to behold, and that this wondrous tree could bring about enlightenment, she grabbed a piece of fruit and ate it. She also offered some to her husband, and he ate it as well.

7 וַתִּפָּקַחְנָה עֵינֵי שְׁנֵיהֶם וַיֵּדְעוּ כִּי עֵירֻמִּם הֵם וַיִּתְפְּרוּ עֲלֵה תְאֵנָה וַיַּעֲשׂוּ לָהֶם חֲגֹרֹת:

7. Then their eyes were opened, and they realized that they were naked. So they sewed fig leaves together and made loincloths for themselves.

What is the first thing that Adam and Eve realize once they eat from the Tree of Knowledge? Why?

How does this knowledge change the relationship between Adam and Eve? How does it change the relationship between Adam, Eve, and God?

13

If you had the chance to undo Adam and Eve's choice to eat of the fruit of the Tree of Knowledge, would you? Would it have been better for humanity to remain in the Garden of Eden by remaining innocent and unaware? Why or why not?

3. Getting "to Know" You

A euphemism is a word used to replace a word that we do not want to say outright. If someone dies for instance, we might say that he or she "passed away." This is a euphemism. The Torah uses a euphemism for sexual intercourse. This is not surprising. The word that is chosen, however, is very surprising.

Genesis 4:1

> א וְהָאָדָם יָדַע אֶת־חַוָּה אִשְׁתּוֹ וַתַּהַר וַתֵּלֶד אֶת־קַיִן וַתֹּאמֶר
> קָנִיתִי אִישׁ אֶת־יְהוָה:

4:1. And the man knew his wife, Eve. She conceived and gave birth to Cain.

What euphemism is being used here for having sex?

There are two different ways to say "knew" in Hebrew. יָדַע (yada) is used if someone had knowledge about something, whereas הִכִּיר (hikir) is used if someone knew a person. It is striking, therefore, that in the passage above, and in the Torah generally, the word יָדַע (yada) is used as a euphemism for sexual intercourse.

Which of the two words, הִכִּיר (hikir) or יָדַע (yada), is the logical choice as a euphemism for making love?

Why do you think the word יָדַע (yada) is used? Does this say anything about the nature of sexuality in the eyes of the Torah? If so, what?

In sexual relations, there is a twofold potential. The great twentieth-century Jewish existential philosopher Martin Buber explains that all of life is lived with this dual potential. We can relate to others as an "It" and treat them as a thing to be used, in what he calls the "I-It" relationship. We can also have moments of true "knowing" in which we fully understand and appreciate the "other." In such moments, we do not want anything from the other; we do not want to exploit him or her, nor do we expect to gain anything from the encounter. This type of relationship Buber calls the "I-Thou."

I and Thou

I and Thou was the seminal work of the great twentieth-century Jewish existential philosopher Martin Buber (1878–1965). In this work, Buber introduces the idea of an I-Thou relationship—a moment of complete understanding, empathy, and appreciation that can exist between two individuals. Buber goes on to suggest that we can experience just such an I-Thou relationship with God. This he termed an I-Eternal Thou relationship. (This text passage is adapted from Martin Buber, *I and Thou*, trans. Walter Kaufmann [Edinburgh: T & T Clark, 1970], page 59.)

I and Thou, Section 2

When I experience another person as a Thou, and have an I-Thou experience with him/her, then s/he is not a thing among things, nor does s/he consist of material qualities. S/he is no longer merely a pronoun (a He or a She), limited by other Hes and Shes, a dot in the universal grid of time and space. Nor is s/he a characteristic that can be experienced and then described. S/he is not merely a loose bundle of labeled qualities. Standing alone and whole, s/he is Thou, and fills my universe. It is not as if there were nothing but s/he. Rather it is as if everything else lives in his/her light.

16

This is true in the same way as a song is not merely a collection of tones, nor a verse a mere collection of words, nor a statute a collection of lines. One must tear and break apart in order to make a unified whole revert back to its component parts. So it is with the person whom I call Thou. I can abstract from him/her the color of his/her hair or the shadings of his/her speech, or the aura of his/her graciousness, and in fact I must often do this, but as soon as I do, s/he is no longer Thou.

In your own words, describe an I-Thou relationship.

What characteristics must an I-Thou relationship or moment have?

According to Buber, an I-Thou relationship is an equal relationship. An I-Thou moment is a moment with no labels. Once you realize you are having one, it is, by definition, over. When you know another as a "Thou," you cannot want to gain anything for yourself from the relationship or to use the other person in any way. When we treat another person as an object, Buber calls this an I-It relationship.

This being the case, why might it be difficult to have an I-Thou sexual relationship?

Might this be more difficult for unmarried teenagers than for married adults? Why or why not?

4. Jacob's Honeymoon

The Torah is filled with love stories. In the following text, Jacob asks Laban for the hand of the beautiful Rachel, with whom he has fallen in love.

Genesis 29:18–28

18 וַיֶּאֱהַב יַעֲקֹב אֶת־רָחֵל וַיֹּאמֶר אֶעֱבָדְךָ שֶׁבַע שָׁנִים בְּרָחֵל בִּתְּךָ הַקְּטַנָּה:

29:18. Jacob loved Rachel, so he said, "I will work for you seven years for Rachel, your younger daughter."

19 וַיֹּאמֶר לָבָן טוֹב תִּתִּי אֹתָהּ לָךְ מִתִּתִּי אֹתָהּ לְאִישׁ אַחֵר שְׁבָה עִמָּדִי:

19. Laban said, "It is better for me that I give her to you than to another man. Stay with me."

20 וַיַּעֲבֹד יַעֲקֹב בְּרָחֵל שֶׁבַע שָׁנִים וַיִּהְיוּ בְעֵינָיו כְּיָמִים אֲחָדִים בְּאַהֲבָתוֹ אֹתָהּ:

20. So Jacob worked seven years for Rachel, but in his eyes the days were few because of his love for her.

21 וַיֹּאמֶר יַעֲקֹב אֶל־לָבָן הָבָה אֶת־אִשְׁתִּי כִּי מָלְאוּ יָמָי וְאָבוֹאָה אֵלֶיהָ:

21. Jacob said to Laban, "Give me my wife, for my days of service are fulfilled, so I may marry her."

22 וַיֶּאֱסֹף לָבָן אֶת־כָּל־אַנְשֵׁי הַמָּקוֹם וַיַּעַשׂ מִשְׁתֶּה:

22. Then Laban gathered all the people of the place and made a feast.

23 וַיְהִי בָעֶרֶב וַיִּקַּח אֶת־לֵאָה בִתּוֹ וַיָּבֵא אֹתָהּ אֵלָיו וַיָּבֹא אֵלֶיהָ:

23. In the evening, he took his daughter Leah and brought her to Jacob, and Jacob lay with her.

24 וַיִּתֵּן לָבָן לָהּ אֶת־זִלְפָּה שִׁפְחָתוֹ לְלֵאָה בִתּוֹ שִׁפְחָה:

24. And Laban gave his maidservant Zilpah to Leah his daughter to be her maidservant.

25 וַיְהִי בַבֹּקֶר וְהִנֵּה־הִוא לֵאָה וַיֹּאמֶר אֶל־לָבָן מַה־זֹּאת עָשִׂיתָ לִּי הֲלֹא בְרָחֵל עָבַדְתִּי עִמָּךְ וְלָמָּה רִמִּיתָנִי:

25. When morning arrived, behold, there was Leah! So Jacob said to Laban, "What is this that you have done to me? Was it not for Rachel that I slaved for you? Why have you deceived me?"

26 וַיֹּאמֶר לָבָן לֹא־יֵעָשֶׂה כֵן בִּמְקוֹמֵנוּ לָתֵת הַצְּעִירָה לִפְנֵי הַבְּכִירָה:

26. Then Laban said, "Such is not the custom in our place, to marry off the younger girl before the older.

27 מַלֵּא שְׁבֻעַ זֹאת וְנִתְּנָה לְךָ גַּם־אֶת־זֹאת בַּעֲבֹדָה אֲשֶׁר תַּעֲבֹד עִמָּדִי עוֹד שֶׁבַע־שָׁנִים אֲחֵרוֹת:

27. Fulfill the bridal week of Leah, and we will give you that one too for the service you will provide me yet another seven years."

28 וַיַּעַשׂ יַעֲקֹב כֵּן וַיְמַלֵּא שְׁבֻעַ זֹאת וַיִּתֶּן־לוֹ אֶת־רָחֵל בִּתּוֹ לוֹ לְאִשָּׁה:

28. So Jacob did so, and the bridal week of Leah was fulfilled, and then he gave him his daughter Rachel as his wife.

Look at verse 25. What is the קֹשִׁי (koshi) here?

Write your own midrash explaining how Jacob could not have known that he was marrying the wrong woman until the next morning.

Could the encounter between Jacob and Leah be considered an I-Thou sexual relationship? Why or why not?

Now let us look at some of the traditional answers to this problem.

B'reishit Rabbah 70:19

ברמשא אתון מעלתא וחפון בוציניא אמר להן מהו כדין
אמרי ליה מה את סבור דאנן דכריך דכוותכון וכל ההוא
ליליא הוה צווח לה רחל והיא עניא ליה בצפרא והנה היא
לאה אמר לה מה רמייתא בת רמאה לאו בליליא הוה
קרינא רחל ואת ענית לי אמרה ליה אית ספר דלית ליה
תלמידים לא כך היה צווח לך אבוך עשו ואת עני ליה.

In the evening, the men of the village came to lead Jacob into the bridal chamber and extinguished the light. "What is the meaning of this?" Jacob demanded. And they replied, "Do you think that we are shameless like you?" All night Jacob called her Rachel, and she answered him. In the morning, however, BEHOLD, THERE WAS LEAH (Genesis 29:25). He said to her, "What is this? You are a deceiver and the daughter of a deceiver!" But Leah retorted, "Is there a teacher without pupils? Did not your father call you Esau and you answered him?"

Leah has a point. Still, just turning the lights out does not seem like it would do the trick. The midrash below goes a bit further in explaining how the subterfuge was accomplished. In deceiving Jacob, it seems, Laban had some inside help.

Talmud

The Talmud is the Oral Law written down. Originally, the Oral Law was committed to memory by the great sages of the day and transmitted from generation to generation by word of mouth; it was never to be written down. By the year 200 C.E., however, it was felt necessary to preserve the Oral Law by committing it to paper. This was called the Mishnah. About 300 years later a commentary on the Mishnah was added, which was called the Gemara. The Mishnah and the Gemara, together with some later commentaries and explanations, make up the Talmud. It is comprised of the debates and legal decisions of the great Rabbis of the period and forms the basis of Rabbinic Judaism to this very day. The Talmud also includes many beautiful midrashim. Two versions of the Talmud exist, one from the community that was in Babylonia (Babylonian Talmud), and the other from the community in Israel (Jerusalem Talmud). We are referring here to the Babylonian Talmud.

Talmud, *M'gillah* 13b

אלא אמר לה: מינסבא לי? אמרה ליה: אין. מידהו, אבא
רמאה הוא, ולא יכלת ליה. — אמר לה: אחיו אנא
ברמאות. — אמרה ליה: ומי שרי לצדיקי לסגויי ברמיותא?
— אמר לה: אין, (שמואל ב' כ"ב) עם נבר תתבר ועם עקש
תתפל. אמר לה: ומאי רמיותא? — אמרה ליה: אית לי
אחתא דקשישא מינאי, ולא מנסיב לי מקמה. מסר לה
סימנים. כי מטא ליליא, אמרה: השתא מיכספא אחתאי,
מסרתינדהו ניהלה. והיינו דכתיב (בראשית כ"ט) ויהי בבקר
והנה היא לאה.

When Jacob asked Rachel to marry him, she replied,
"Yes, I will! But my father is a trickster, and he will outwit
you." He replied, "I am his brother in trickery." To which
she responded, "Is it permissible for the righteous to
indulge in deception?" "Yes," he replied, "with the pure
you must be pure, and with the crooked you must be
cunning. What is his trickery?" She replied, "I have an
older sister, and he will not let me marry before her."
Upon hearing this, Jacob gave Rachel certain secret signs.
But when night came, she said to herself, "My older sister
will be put to shame." So she gave the secret signs to Leah.
And the next morning, BEHOLD, THERE WAS LEAH
(Genesis 29:25).

*Is this realistic? Why would Rachel do this for her sister? What would
you have done in her place?*

*Describe an experience in your own life in which deception was used as
the basis of a relationship. How did the relationship fare?*

Our ancestors probably lived in a way very similar to the Bedouin in the Middle East today. This is a picture of a Bedouin bride.

© Laura Zito, Photo Researchers

Does this picture give you any additional ideas about how Jacob could have been fooled?

5. The Black Hat and the Well

Where does one go to find the proper mate? In the Torah it seems that if you wanted to meet your own true love, you would head right on down to the local watering hole. No, not the singles' bar, but rather the actual watering hole, the well. How remarkable that the wives of Isaac, Jacob, and Moses were all found at wells!

Sometimes we find motifs in the Torah, such as the well, that seem to jump from one character to another. According to the Documentary Hypothesis, this is called "the migration of myth."

In fact, this sort of thing happens in real life. Imagine that there is a rumor going around town that a tall dentist named Dr. Smith is having an extramarital affair with a short lawyer named Mrs. Jones. By the time the rumor has run its course, people will be saying that it is actually Dr. Jones, a short podiatrist, who is cheating on his wife. The original myth "migrates" from one person to another.

Have you ever experienced this phenomenon of the "migration of myth" in your own life? When?

The Documentary Hypothesis, however, is not accepted by all. The traditional perspective, in which every single word of the Torah is thought to be literally true, stands in opposition to the Documentary Hypothesis.

Based on the traditional perspective, how would you explain the coincidence of the well?

There is one additional explanation for this migration of myth that is quite intriguing. It is provided in an article entitled "Biblical Type Scenes and the Uses of Convention" by Robert Alter (*The Art of*

Biblical Narrative, 1981). He believes that the scenes at the well are examples of a literary device called the "betrothal type-scene."

What is a literary device? Imagine that you have just entered a movie theater. The lights go out, the movie begins, and suddenly on screen you see a cowboy with a black hat. *What do you immediately know about him?*

The black hat is a literary device. Once we see it, we know something about the character: he is the "bad guy." We even know what will happen to him in the end.

It is not as simple as that, however. Imagine now that the black hat is a small black fedora instead of a cowboy hat. Immediately you know that this bad guy is a dandy and a gambler who undoubtedly carries a small, concealed pistol instead of two big six-shooters. If the rim of the black hat is flat instead of curling upward, you know that this "bad guy" is from south of the border. If he is also wearing a mask, you will often find that he is actually a hero who has been labeled unfairly as an outlaw by the authorities. So, not only can a literary device help us know who the characters are and what is likely to happen to them, it can also reveal subtle shadings of their personalities. In biblical literature, the well functions like the black hat. Once we see it, we know that someone is about to get married. The way the well scene is described, however, may tell us a great deal more about the characters involved and about their relationship. With this in mind, compare and contrast the following betrothal stories from the Torah.

Genesis 24:10–33, 49–61

10 וַיִּקַּח הָעֶבֶד עֲשָׂרָה גְמַלִּים מִגְּמַלֵּי אֲדֹנָיו וַיֵּלֶךְ וְכָל־טוּב
אֲדֹנָיו בְּיָדוֹ וַיָּקָם וַיֵּלֶךְ אֶל־אֲרַם נַהֲרַיִם אֶל־עִיר נָחוֹר:

24:10. Then the servant took ten camels from his master's herd and set out with a sizable dowry from his master in his hand, and rose and made his way to Aram-Naharaim, to the city of Nahor.

וַיַּבְרֵךְ הַגְּמַלִּים מִחוּץ לָעִיר אֶל־בְּאֵר הַמָּיִם לְעֵת עֶרֶב לְעֵת 11
צֵאת הַשֹּׁאֲבֹת:

11. He made the camels kneel down outside the city by the well at evening time, the time when women come out to draw water.

וַיֹּאמַר יְהוָה אֱלֹהֵי אֲדֹנִי אַבְרָהָם הַקְרֵה־נָא לְפָנַי הַיּוֹם 12
וַעֲשֵׂה־חֶסֶד עִם אֲדֹנִי אַבְרָהָם:

12. And he said, "*Adonai,* God of my master Abraham, may You grant me good fortune today and deal graciously with my master Abraham.

הִנֵּה אָנֹכִי נִצָּב עַל־עֵין הַמָּיִם וּבְנוֹת אַנְשֵׁי הָעִיר יֹצְאֹת 13
לִשְׁאֹב מָיִם:

13. Here I am, standing by the spring of water, and the daughters of the people of the town are coming out to draw water.

וְהָיָה הַנַּעֲרָה אֲשֶׁר אֹמַר אֵלֶיהָ הַטִּי־נָא כַדֵּךְ וְאֶשְׁתֶּה 14
וְאָמְרָה שְׁתֵה וְגַם־גְּמַלֶּיךָ אַשְׁקֶה אֹתָהּ הֹכַחְתָּ לְעַבְדְּךָ לְיִצְחָק
וּבָהּ אֵדַע כִּי־עָשִׂיתָ חֶסֶד עִם־אֲדֹנִי:

14. Let it be that the maiden to whom I say, 'Please, lower your jar so I may drink,' will reply, 'Drink, and I will also water your camels.' She will be the one You have designated for Your servant Isaac. Thereby I will know through her that You have dealt graciously with my master."

15 וַיְהִי־הוּא טֶרֶם כִּלָּה לְדַבֵּר וְהִנֵּה רִבְקָה יֹצֵאת אֲשֶׁר יֻלְּדָה לִבְתוּאֵל בֶּן־מִלְכָּה אֵשֶׁת נָחוֹר אֲחִי אַבְרָהָם וְכַדָּהּ עַל־שִׁכְמָהּ:

15. He had barely finished speaking when Rebekah, who was born of Bethuel, the son of Milcah the wife of Abraham's brother Nahor, appeared with her jar on her shoulder.

16 וְהַנַּעֲרָה טֹבַת מַרְאֶה מְאֹד בְּתוּלָה וְאִישׁ לֹא יְדָעָהּ וַתֵּרֶד הָעַיְנָה וַתְּמַלֵּא כַדָּהּ וַתָּעַל:

16. The maiden was very beautiful, a virgin whom no man had known. She went down to the spring, filled her jar, and came up.

17 וַיָּרָץ הָעֶבֶד לִקְרָאתָהּ וַיֹּאמֶר הַגְמִיאִינִי נָא מְעַט־מַיִם מִכַּדֵּךְ:

17. The servant ran toward her and said, "Please, let me sip a little water from your jar."

18 וַתֹּאמֶר שְׁתֵה אֲדֹנִי וַתְּמַהֵר וַתֹּרֶד כַּדָּהּ עַל־יָדָהּ וַתַּשְׁקֵהוּ:

18. She said, "Drink, my lord," and quickly lowered her jar on her hand, allowing him to drink.

19 וַתְּכַל לְהַשְׁקֹתוֹ וַתֹּאמֶר גַּם לִגְמַלֶּיךָ אֶשְׁאָב עַד אִם־כִּלּוּ לִשְׁתֹּת:

19. When she had enabled him to drink his fill, she said, "I will also draw water for your camels until they are sated."

20 וַתְּמַהֵר וַתְּעַר כַּדָּהּ אֶל־הַשֹּׁקֶת וַתָּרָץ עוֹד אֶל־הַבְּאֵר לִשְׁאֹב וַתִּשְׁאַב לְכָל־גְּמַלָּיו:

20. So she hurried and emptied her jar into the trough. Then she ran back to the well to draw water, and she did so for all of his camels.

21 וְהָאִישׁ מִשְׁתָּאֵה לָהּ מַחֲרִישׁ לָדַעַת הַהִצְלִיחַ יְהוָה דַּרְכּוֹ אִם־לֹא:

21. The man stood gazing at her silently, waiting to know whether *Adonai* had made his journey successful or not.

22 וַיְהִי כַּאֲשֶׁר כִּלּוּ הַגְּמַלִּים לִשְׁתּוֹת וַיִּקַּח הָאִישׁ נֶזֶם זָהָב בֶּקַע מִשְׁקָלוֹ וּשְׁנֵי צְמִידִים עַל־יָדֶיהָ עֲשָׂרָה זָהָב מִשְׁקָלָם:

22. When the camels had finished drinking, the man took a golden nose ring weighing a *beka* [about half a shekel] and two gold bracelets for her arms, ten shekels in weight.

23 וַיֹּאמֶר בַּת־מִי אַתְּ הַגִּידִי נָא לִי הֲיֵשׁ בֵּית־אָבִיךְ מָקוֹם לָנוּ לָלִין:

23. And he said, "Whose daughter are you? Please tell me, is there room in your father's house for us to spend the night?"

24 וַתֹּאמֶר אֵלָיו בַּת־בְּתוּאֵל אָנֹכִי בֶּן־מִלְכָּה אֲשֶׁר יָלְדָה לְנָחוֹר:

24. She said to him, "I am the daughter of Bethuel, the son of Milcah, whom she bore to Nahor."

25 וַתֹּאמֶר אֵלָיו גַּם־תֶּבֶן גַּם־מִסְפּוֹא רַב עִמָּנוּ גַּם־מָקוֹם לָלוּן:

25. And she said to him, "There is plenty of straw and feed at home, and also room to spend the night."

26 וַיִּקֹּד הָאִישׁ וַיִּשְׁתַּחוּ לַיהוָה:

26. So the man prostrated himself before *Adonai.*

27 וַיֹּאמֶר בָּרוּךְ יְהוָה אֱלֹהֵי אֲדֹנִי אַבְרָהָם אֲשֶׁר לֹא־עָזַב חַסְדּוֹ
וַאֲמִתּוֹ מֵעִם אֲדֹנִי אָנֹכִי בַּדֶּרֶךְ נָחַנִי יְהוָה בֵּית אֲחֵי אֲדֹנִי:

27. He said, "Blessed be *Adonai,* God of my master Abraham, who has not withheld his kindness and truth from my master. I have been guided on my journey by *Adonai* to the house of my master's brothers."

28 וַתָּרָץ הַנַּעֲרָה וַתַּגֵּד לְבֵית אִמָּהּ כַּדְּבָרִים הָאֵלֶּה:

28. The maiden ran to tell all these things to her mother's household.

29 וּלְרִבְקָה אָח וּשְׁמוֹ לָבָן וַיָּרָץ לָבָן אֶל־הָאִישׁ הַחוּצָה
אֶל־הָעָיִן:

29. Rebekah had a brother whose name was Laban. Laban ran to the man at the spring.

30 וַיְהִי כִּרְאֹת אֶת־הַנֶּזֶם וְאֶת־הַצְּמִדִים עַל־יְדֵי אֲחֹתוֹ וּכְשָׁמְעוֹ
אֶת־דִּבְרֵי רִבְקָה אֲחֹתוֹ לֵאמֹר כֹּה־דִבֶּר אֵלַי הָאִישׁ וַיָּבֹא אֶל־
הָאִישׁ וְהִנֵּה עֹמֵד עַל־הַגְּמַלִּים עַל־הָעָיִן:

30. Upon seeing the nose ring and the bracelets on his sister's arms, and upon hearing his sister Rebekah's words saying, "Thus the man spoke to me," he went to the man who was standing near the camels by the spring.

31 וַיֹּאמֶר בּוֹא בְּרוּךְ יְהוָה לָמָּה תַעֲמֹד בַּחוּץ וְאָנֹכִי פִּנִּיתִי
הַבַּיִת וּמָקוֹם לַגְּמַלִּים:

31. He said, "Come, O blessed of *Adonai.* Why do you stand outside when I have prepared the house for you, and a place for the camels as well?"

32 וַיָּבֹא הָאִישׁ הַבַּיְתָה וַיְפַתַּח הַגְּמַלִּים וַיִּתֵּן תֶּבֶן וּמִסְפּוֹא לַגְּמַלִּים וּמַיִם לִרְחֹץ רַגְלָיו וְרַגְלֵי הָאֲנָשִׁים אֲשֶׁר אִתּוֹ:

32. So the man entered the house and unloaded the camels. He gave the camels straw, and feed, and brought water to wash the servant's legs and the legs of the people who were with him.

33 וַיּוּשַׂם לְפָנָיו לֶאֱכֹל וַיֹּאמֶר לֹא אֹכַל עַד אִם־דִּבַּרְתִּי דְּבָרָי וַיֹּאמֶר דַּבֵּר:

33. And food was placed before him to eat, but he said, "I will not eat until I have told my tale." And his host said, "Speak."

Abraham's servant then takes the next thirteen verses (a great deal of text for the normally terse Book of Genesis) to repeat the story of his quest to Laban in exacting detail. He concludes by saying:

49 וְעַתָּה אִם־יֶשְׁכֶם עֹשִׂים חֶסֶד וֶאֱמֶת אֶת־אֲדֹנִי הַגִּידוּ לִי וְאִם־לֹא הַגִּידוּ לִי וְאֶפְנֶה עַל־יָמִין אוֹ עַל־שְׂמֹאל:

49. "And now, if you mean to treat my master in kindness and truth, tell me, and if not, tell me as well, that I may turn right and left."

50 וַיַּעַן לָבָן וּבְתוּאֵל וַיֹּאמְרוּ מֵיְהוָה יָצָא הַדָּבָר לֹא נוּכַל דַּבֵּר אֵלֶיךָ רַע אוֹ־טוֹב:

50. Then Laban and Bethuel answered and said, "The matter came from *Adonai*. We can say to you neither good nor bad.

51 הִנֵּה־רִבְקָה לְפָנֶיךָ קַח וָלֵךְ וּתְהִי אִשָּׁה לְבֶן־אֲדֹנֶיךָ כַּאֲשֶׁר דִּבֶּר יְהוָה:

51. Here is Rebekah before you, take her and go, and let her be a wife to the son of your master as *Adonai* has spoken.''

52 וַיְהִי כַּאֲשֶׁר שָׁמַע עֶבֶד אַבְרָהָם אֶת־דִּבְרֵיהֶם וַיִּשְׁתַּחוּ אַרְצָה לַיהוָה:

52. When Abraham's servant heard their words, he bowed low to the ground before *Adonai*.

53 וַיּוֹצֵא הָעֶבֶד כְּלֵי־כֶסֶף וּכְלֵי זָהָב וּבְגָדִים וַיִּתֵּן לְרִבְקָה וּמִגְדָּנֹת נָתַן לְאָחִיהָ וּלְאִמָּהּ:

53. The servant brought objects of silver and gold, and garments, and gave them to Rebekah, and presents to her brother and mother.

54 וַיֹּאכְלוּ וַיִּשְׁתּוּ הוּא וְהָאֲנָשִׁים אֲשֶׁר־עִמּוֹ וַיָּלִינוּ וַיָּקוּמוּ בַבֹּקֶר וַיֹּאמֶר שַׁלְּחֻנִי לַאדֹנִי:

54. They ate and drank, he and the people that were with him, and they spent the night. When they arose in the morning, he said, ''Send me to my master.''

55 וַיֹּאמֶר אָחִיהָ וְאִמָּהּ תֵּשֵׁב הַנַּעֲרָה אִתָּנוּ יָמִים אוֹ עָשׂוֹר אַחַר תֵּלֵךְ:

55. Her brother and mother said, ''Let the maiden remain with us some ten days; then she will go.''

56 וַיֹּאמֶר אֲלֵהֶם אַל־תְּאַחֲרוּ אֹתִי וַיהוָה הִצְלִיחַ דַּרְכִּי שַׁלְּחוּנִי
וְאֵלְכָה לַאדֹנִי:

56. And he said to them, "Do not delay me now that *Adonai* has made my journey successful. Give me leave to go to my master."

57 וַיֹּאמְרוּ נִקְרָא לַנַּעֲרָה וְנִשְׁאֲלָה אֶת־פִּיהָ:

57. And they said, "Let us call the maiden and ask for the answer from her own mouth."

58 וַיִּקְרְאוּ לְרִבְקָה וַיֹּאמְרוּ אֵלֶיהָ הֲתֵלְכִי עִם־הָאִישׁ הַזֶּה
וַתֹּאמֶר אֵלֵךְ:

58. And they called to Rebekah and they said to her, "Will you go with the man?" And she said, "I will go."

59 וַיְשַׁלְּחוּ אֶת־רִבְקָה אֲחֹתָם וְאֶת־מֵנִקְתָּהּ וְאֶת־עֶבֶד אַבְרָהָם
וְאֶת־אֲנָשָׁיו:

59. So they sent Rebekah their sister and her nurse, as well as Abraham's servant and his men.

60 וַיְבָרֲכוּ אֶת־רִבְקָה וַיֹּאמְרוּ לָהּ
אֲחֹתֵנוּ
אַתְּ הֲיִי
לְאַלְפֵי רְבָבָה
וְיִירַשׁ
זַרְעֵךְ
אֵת שַׁעַר שֹׂנְאָיו:

60. They blessed Rebekah and said to her, "Our sister, may you come to be thousands of myriads, and may your offspring seize the gates of their foes."

וַתָּקָם רִבְקָה וְנַעֲרֹתֶיהָ וַתִּרְכַּבְנָה עַל־הַגְּמַלִּים וַתֵּלַכְנָה 61
אַחֲרֵי הָאִישׁ וַיִּקַּח הָעֶבֶד אֶת־רִבְקָה וַיֵּלַךְ:

61. Then Rebekah and her maids arose, mounted their
camels, and followed the man. The servant took Rebekah
and went.

*Where is Isaac in this story? What might his absence say about his
personality?*

*This passage is much longer than those that follow. It is repetitive,
stately, formal, and slow. Does this fit with what you know about Isaac's
life before and after his marriage to Rebekah?*

*What does Isaac's absence from his own courtship imply about his
marriage?*

Now contrast Isaac's slow, formal, and distant betrothal with that of his
son Jacob.

Genesis 29:1–20

וַיִּשָּׂא יַעֲקֹב רַגְלָיו וַיֵּלֶךְ אַרְצָה בְנֵי־קֶדֶם: 1

29:1. Jacob rose to his feet and went toward the land of the
inhabitants of the East.

וַיַּרְא וְהִנֵּה בְאֵר בַּשָּׂדֶה וְהִנֵּה־שָׁם שְׁלֹשָׁה עֶדְרֵי־צֹאן רֹבְצִים 2
עָלֶיהָ כִּי מִן־הַבְּאֵר הַהִוא יַשְׁקוּ הָעֲדָרִים וְהָאֶבֶן גְּדֹלָה עַל־פִּי
הַבְּאֵר:

2. He looked and there was a well in the field. And there
were three flocks of sheep lying there beside it, and from
that well they would water their flocks. The stone on the
mouth of the well was large.

33

3 וְנֶאֶסְפוּ־שָׁמָּה כָל־הָעֲדָרִים וְגָלֲלוּ אֶת־הָאֶבֶן מֵעַל פִּי הַבְּאֵר
וְהִשְׁקוּ אֶת־הַצֹּאן וְהֵשִׁיבוּ אֶת־הָאֶבֶן עַל־פִּי הַבְּאֵר לִמְקֹמָהּ:

3. The flocks would be gathered there, and they would roll
the stone from the mouth of the well and water the sheep.
Then they would return the stone to its place over the
mouth of the well.

4 וַיֹּאמֶר לָהֶם יַעֲקֹב אַחַי מֵאַיִן אַתֶּם וַיֹּאמְרוּ מֵחָרָן אֲנָחְנוּ:

4. Jacob said to them, "My brothers, where are you
from?" And they said, "We are from Haran."

5 וַיֹּאמֶר לָהֶם הַיְדַעְתֶּם אֶת־לָבָן בֶּן־נָחוֹר וַיֹּאמְרוּ יָדָעְנוּ:

5. He said to them, "Do you know Laban the son of
Nahor?" And they said, "We know him."

6 וַיֹּאמֶר לָהֶם הֲשָׁלוֹם לוֹ וַיֹּאמְרוּ שָׁלוֹם וְהִנֵּה רָחֵל בִּתּוֹ בָּאָה
עִם־הַצֹּאן:

6. He said to them, "Is he well?" And they said, "He is
well, and here is his daughter Rachel coming with the
sheep."

7 וַיֹּאמֶר הֵן עוֹד הַיּוֹם גָּדוֹל לֹא־עֵת הֵאָסֵף הַמִּקְנֶה הַשְׁקוּ
הַצֹּאן וּלְכוּ רְעוּ:

7. And he said, "It is still broad daylight; it is not yet time
to gather the flock. Water the animals, and take them to
pasture."

8 וַיֹּאמְרוּ לֹא נוּכַל עַד אֲשֶׁר יֵאָסְפוּ כָּל־הָעֲדָרִים וְגָלֲלוּ
אֶת־הָאֶבֶן מֵעַל פִּי הַבְּאֵר וְהִשְׁקִינוּ הַצֹּאן:

8. But they said, "We cannot do so until the flocks are
gathered and the stone is rolled from the mouth of the
well. Then we will water the sheep."

9 עוֹדֶנּוּ מְדַבֵּר עִמָּם וְרָחֵל בָּאָה עִם־הַצֹּאן אֲשֶׁר לְאָבִיהָ כִּי
רֹעָה הִוא:

9. He was still speaking with them when Rachel came up
with her father's flock, for she was a shepherdess.

10 וַיְהִי כַּאֲשֶׁר רָאָה יַעֲקֹב אֶת־רָחֵל בַּת־לָבָן אֲחִי אִמּוֹ
וְאֶת־צֹאן לָבָן אֲחִי אִמּוֹ וַיִּגַּשׁ יַעֲקֹב וַיָּגֶל אֶת־הָאֶבֶן מֵעַל פִּי
הַבְּאֵר וַיַּשְׁקְ אֶת־צֹאן לָבָן אֲחִי אִמּוֹ:

10. And when Jacob saw Rachel, the daughter of Laban,
his mother's brother, and the sheep of Laban his uncle,
Jacob approached and rolled the stone from the mouth of
the well and watered the flock of his uncle Laban.

11 וַיִּשַּׁק יַעֲקֹב לְרָחֵל וַיִּשָּׂא אֶת־קֹלוֹ וַיֵּבְךְּ:

11. Then Jacob kissed Rachel; and he raised his voice and
he wept.

12 וַיַּגֵּד יַעֲקֹב לְרָחֵל כִּי אֲחִי אָבִיהָ הוּא וְכִי בֶן־רִבְקָה הוּא
וַתָּרָץ וַתַּגֵּד לְאָבִיהָ:

12. Jacob told Rachel that he was her father's relative, that
he was Rebekah's son. She then ran and told her father.

13 וַיְהִי כִשְׁמֹעַ לָבָן אֶת־שֵׁמַע יַעֲקֹב בֶּן־אֲחֹתוֹ וַיָּרָץ לִקְרָאתוֹ
וַיְחַבֶּק־לוֹ וַיְנַשֶּׁק־לוֹ וַיְבִיאֵהוּ אֶל־בֵּיתוֹ וַיְסַפֵּר לְלָבָן אֵת
כָּל־הַדְּבָרִים הָאֵלֶּה:

13. Upon hearing the news of Jacob, his sister's son, he ran
to greet him, embraced him, kissed him, and took him into
his house. He told Laban all these things.

14 וַיֹּאמֶר לוֹ לָבָן אַךְ עַצְמִי וּבְשָׂרִי אָתָּה וַיֵּשֶׁב עִמּוֹ חֹדֶשׁ יָמִים:

14. Then Laban said to him, "You are of my bone and of my flesh." And Jacob stayed with Laban for one month.

15 וַיֹּאמֶר לָבָן לְיַעֲקֹב הֲכִי־אָחִי אַתָּה וַעֲבַדְתַּנִי חִנָּם הַגִּידָה לִּי מַה־מַּשְׂכֻּרְתֶּךָ:

15. Then Laban said to Jacob, "Just because you are my relative, should you work for me for free? Tell me, what are your wages?"

16 וּלְלָבָן שְׁתֵּי בָנוֹת שֵׁם הַגְּדֹלָה לֵאָה וְשֵׁם הַקְּטַנָּה רָחֵל:

16. Laban had two daughters. The name of the older one was Leah, and the name of the younger one was Rachel.

17 וְעֵינֵי לֵאָה רַכּוֹת וְרָחֵל הָיְתָה יְפַת־תֹּאַר וִיפַת מַרְאֶה:

17. Leah was unattractive, but Rachel was shapely and beautiful to look upon.

18 וַיֶּאֱהַב יַעֲקֹב אֶת־רָחֵל וַיֹּאמֶר אֶעֱבָדְךָ שֶׁבַע שָׁנִים בְּרָחֵל בִּתְּךָ הַקְּטַנָּה:

18. Jacob loved Rachel, and he said to Laban, "I will work for you for seven years for your younger daughter Rachel."

19 וַיֹּאמֶר לָבָן טוֹב תִּתִּי אֹתָהּ לָךְ מִתִּתִּי אֹתָהּ לְאִישׁ אַחֵר שְׁבָה עִמָּדִי:

19. Then Laban said, "Better that I give her to you than to another man. Stay with me."

20 וַיַּעֲבֹד יַעֲקֹב בְּרָחֵל שֶׁבַע שָׁנִים וַיִּהְיוּ בְעֵינָיו כְּיָמִים אֲחָדִים בְּאַהֲבָתוֹ אֹתָהּ:

20. And Jacob worked for Rachel for seven years, and they seemed to him but a few days because of his love for her.

Notice here that Jacob goes right up and kisses Rachel.

What does this say about his personality?

What do you think the relationship between Jacob and Rachel might have been like?

Jacob also wrestles the rock off the well so that she can drink.

Can you think of anywhere else in the Torah where Jacob wrestles?

Can you think of anywhere else in the Torah where Jacob is associated with rocks?

In what way do these rocky, wrestling moments act as clues about his character?

The myth of the well is not restricted to the Book of Genesis. In Exodus we find the betrothal type-scene as well.

Exodus 2:15–21

15 וַיִּשְׁמַע פַּרְעֹה אֶת־הַדָּבָר הַזֶּה וַיְבַקֵּשׁ לַהֲרֹג אֶת־מֹשֶׁה וַיִּבְרַח מֹשֶׁה מִפְּנֵי פַרְעֹה וַיֵּשֶׁב בְּאֶרֶץ־מִדְיָן וַיֵּשֶׁב עַל־הַבְּאֵר:

2:15. When Pharaoh learned that Moses had stricken the taskmaster, he set out to kill Moses. But Moses fled from Pharaoh, arriving in the land of Midian. There he sat down beside a well.

16 וּלְכֹהֵן מִדְיָן שֶׁבַע בָּנוֹת וַתָּבֹאנָה וַתִּדְלֶנָה וַתְּמַלֶּאנָה אֶת־הָרְהָטִים לְהַשְׁקוֹת צֹאן אֲבִיהֶן:

16. And the priest of Midian had seven daughters. They came to draw water and filled the troughs to water their father's flock.

17 וַיָּבֹאוּ הָרֹעִים וַיְגָרְשׁוּם וַיָּקָם מֹשֶׁה וַיּוֹשִׁעָן וַיַּשְׁקְ אֶת־צֹאנָם:

17. But shepherds came and drove them off. Moses rose up and rescued them, and he watered their flock.

18 וַתָּבֹאנָה אֶל־רְעוּאֵל אֲבִיהֶן וַיֹּאמֶר מַדּוּעַ מִהַרְתֶּן בֹּא הַיּוֹם:

18. When they returned to their father, Reuel [also known as Jethro], he said, "How is it that you have returned so early today?"

19 וַתֹּאמַרְןָ אִישׁ מִצְרִי הִצִּילָנוּ מִיַּד הָרֹעִים וְגַם־דָּלֹה דָלָה לָנוּ וַיַּשְׁקְ אֶת־הַצֹּאן:

19. She responded, "An Egyptian saved us from the shepherds. He even drew water for us and watered the flock."

20 וַיֹּאמֶר אֶל־בְּנֹתָיו וְאַיּוֹ לָמָּה זֶּה עֲזַבְתֶּן אֶת־הָאִישׁ קִרְאֶן לוֹ וְיֹאכַל לָחֶם:

20. He said to his daughters, "Where is he then? Why did you abandon the man? Invite him to break bread with us."

21 וַיּוֹאֶל מֹשֶׁה לָשֶׁבֶת אֶת־הָאִישׁ וַיִּתֵּן אֶת־צִפֹּרָה בִתּוֹ לְמֹשֶׁה:

21. Moses agreed to reside with this man, who gave Moses his daughter Zipporah for a wife.

How is Moses' wife chosen for him?

What does this say about his relationship with Zipporah? How does this differ from the bond between Jacob and Rachel?

Moses fights off the "bad guys" and is rewarded by his father-in-law with a seemingly anonymous daughter. There is no courtship whatsoever.

What might this indicate about Zipporah's role in Moses' life?

Is this typical of the spouse of a great political leader?

Would it be difficult to be married to Moses? What about a modern-day leader, like the president of the United States or the rabbi of your congregation? Why or why not?

6. The Rape of Dinah

Two wrongs do not always make a right. In the midst of the love stories of Genesis, we find this disturbing vignette.

Genesis 34:1–24

א וַתֵּצֵא דִינָה בַּת־לֵאָה אֲשֶׁר יָלְדָה לְיַעֲקֹב לִרְאוֹת בִּבְנוֹת הָאָרֶץ:

34:1. And Dinah, the daughter of Leah, whom she bore to Jacob, went out to see the daughters of the land.

ב וַיַּרְא אֹתָהּ שְׁכֶם בֶּן־חֲמוֹר הַחִוִּי נְשִׂיא הָאָרֶץ וַיִּקַּח אֹתָהּ וַיִּשְׁכַּב אֹתָהּ וַיְעַנֶּהָ:

2. And when Shechem, the son of Hamor the Hivite, prince of the country, saw her, he took her, and lay with her, and defiled her.

ג וַתִּדְבַּק נַפְשׁוֹ בְּדִינָה בַּת־יַעֲקֹב וַיֶּאֱהַב אֶת־הַנַּעֲרָה וַיְדַבֵּר עַל־לֵב הַנַּעֲרָה:

3. And his soul was drawn to Dinah, the daughter of Jacob, and he loved the girl and spoke lovingly to her.

ד וַיֹּאמֶר שְׁכֶם אֶל־חֲמוֹר אָבִיו לֵאמֹר קַח־לִי אֶת־הַיַּלְדָּה הַזֹּאת לְאִשָּׁה:

4. And Shechem spoke to his father Hamor, saying, "You must get me this girl for a wife."

40

וַיַּעֲקֹב שָׁמַע כִּי טִמֵּא אֶת־דִּינָה בִתּוֹ וּבָנָיו הָיוּ אֶת־מִקְנֵהוּ 5
בַּשָּׂדֶה וְהֶחֱרִשׁ יַעֲקֹב עַד־בֹּאָם:

5. When Jacob heard that he had defiled Dinah his daughter, his sons were with the cattle out in the fields, so Jacob held his peace until they came.

וַיֵּצֵא חֲמוֹר אֲבִי־שְׁכֶם אֶל־יַעֲקֹב לְדַבֵּר אִתּוֹ: 6

6. Hamor, the father of Shechem, went out to Jacob to speak with him.

וּבְנֵי יַעֲקֹב בָּאוּ מִן־הַשָּׂדֶה כְּשָׁמְעָם וַיִּתְעַצְּבוּ הָאֲנָשִׁים וַיִּחַר 7
לָהֶם מְאֹד כִּי־נְבָלָה עָשָׂה בְיִשְׂרָאֵל לִשְׁכַּב אֶת־בַּת־יַעֲקֹב וְכֵן
לֹא יֵעָשֶׂה:

7. When the sons of Jacob came in from the field and heard what had happened, they were outraged and exceedingly angry, because he had done a despicable thing in Israel, lying with Jacob's daughter, a thing not to be done.

וַיְדַבֵּר חֲמוֹר אִתָּם לֵאמֹר שְׁכֶם בְּנִי חָשְׁקָה נַפְשׁוֹ בְּבִתְּכֶם תְּנוּ 8
נָא אֹתָהּ לוֹ לְאִשָּׁה:

8. And Hamor spoke with them, saying, "The soul of my son Shechem longs for your daughter. I beg you give her to him for a wife.

וְהִתְחַתְּנוּ אֹתָנוּ בְּנֹתֵיכֶם תִּתְּנוּ־לָנוּ וְאֶת־בְּנֹתֵינוּ תִּקְחוּ לָכֶם: 9

9. Intermarry with us, and give your daughters to us, and take our daughters for yourselves.

10 וְאִתָּנוּ תֵּשֵׁבוּ וְהָאָרֶץ תִּהְיֶה לִפְנֵיכֶם שְׁבוּ וּסְחָרוּהָ וְהֵאָחֲזוּ בָּהּ:

10. And you shall live with us, and the land shall lie before you. Live and trade in it, and become wealthy in it."

11 וַיֹּאמֶר שְׁכֶם אֶל־אָבִיהָ וְאֶל־אַחֶיהָ אֶמְצָא־חֵן בְּעֵינֵיכֶם וַאֲשֶׁר תֹּאמְרוּ אֵלַי אֶתֵּן:

11. Then Shechem said to her father and to her brothers, "Do this favor for me, and whatever you shall ask of me I will give.

12 הַרְבּוּ עָלַי מְאֹד מֹהַר וּמַתָּן וְאֶתְּנָה כַּאֲשֶׁר תֹּאמְרוּ אֵלָי וּתְנוּ־לִי אֶת־הַנַּעֲרָה לְאִשָּׁה:

12. Demand of me a dowry, as well as gifts, and I will give you whatever you say. Just give me the girl for a wife."

13 וַיַּעֲנוּ בְנֵי־יַעֲקֹב אֶת־שְׁכֶם וְאֶת־חֲמוֹר אָבִיו בְּמִרְמָה וַיְדַבֵּרוּ אֲשֶׁר טִמֵּא אֵת דִּינָה אֲחֹתָם:

13. And the sons of Jacob answered Shechem and Hamor his father deceitfully, because he had defiled Dinah their sister,

14 וַיֹּאמְרוּ אֲלֵיהֶם לֹא נוּכַל לַעֲשׂוֹת הַדָּבָר הַזֶּה לָתֵת אֶת־אֲחֹתֵנוּ לְאִישׁ אֲשֶׁר־לוֹ עָרְלָה כִּי־חֶרְפָּה הִוא לָנוּ:

14. Saying, "We cannot do this thing, to give our sister to one who is uncircumcised, for that would be a disgrace among us.

15 אַךְ־בְּזֹאת נֵאוֹת לָכֶם אִם תִּהְיוּ כָמֹנוּ לְהִמֹּל לָכֶם כָּל־זָכָר:

15. Only on this condition will we accede to your request: that every male among you be circumcised.

16 וְנָתַנּוּ אֶת־בְּנֹתֵינוּ לָכֶם וְאֶת־בְּנֹתֵיכֶם נִקַּח־לָנוּ וְיָשַׁבְנוּ
אִתְּכֶם וְהָיִינוּ לְעַם אֶחָד:

16. Then will we give our daughters to you, and we will take your daughters to us, and we will live with you, and we will become one people.

17 וְאִם־לֹא תִשְׁמְעוּ אֵלֵינוּ לְהִמּוֹל וְלָקַחְנוּ אֶת־בִּתֵּנוּ וְהָלָכְנוּ:

17. But if you will not listen to us, to be circumcised, then we will take our daughter, and we will go."

18 וַיִּיטְבוּ דִבְרֵיהֶם בְּעֵינֵי חֲמוֹר וּבְעֵינֵי שְׁכֶם בֶּן־חֲמוֹר:

18. Their words pleased Hamor and Shechem his son.

19 וְלֹא־אֵחַר הַנַּעַר לַעֲשׂוֹת הַדָּבָר כִּי חָפֵץ בְּבַת־יַעֲקֹב וְהוּא
נִכְבָּד מִכֹּל בֵּית אָבִיו:

19. And the young man did not hesitate to do this thing, because he took delight in Jacob's daughter. He was most respected in the community,

20 וַיָּבֹא חֲמוֹר וּשְׁכֶם בְּנוֹ אֶל־שַׁעַר עִירָם וַיְדַבְּרוּ אֶל־אַנְשֵׁי
עִירָם לֵאמֹר:

20. So Hamor and Shechem his son came to the gate of their city and talked with the men of their city, saying,

21 הָאֲנָשִׁים הָאֵלֶּה שְׁלֵמִים הֵם אִתָּנוּ וְיֵשְׁבוּ בָאָרֶץ וְיִסְחֲרוּ
אֹתָהּ וְהָאָרֶץ הִנֵּה רַחֲבַת־יָדַיִם לִפְנֵיהֶם אֶת־בְּנֹתָם נִקַּח־לָנוּ
לְנָשִׁים וְאֶת־בְּנֹתֵינוּ נִתֵּן לָהֶם:

21. "These men are peaceable with us. Therefore let them live in the land and trade in it, for behold the land is large enough for them. Let us take their daughters to us for wives, and let us give them our daughters.

22 אַךְ־בְּזֹאת יֵאֹתוּ לָנוּ הָאֲנָשִׁים לָשֶׁבֶת אִתָּנוּ לִהְיוֹת לְעַם
אֶחָד בְּהִמּוֹל לָנוּ כָּל־זָכָר כַּאֲשֶׁר הֵם נִמֹּלִים:

22. The only way that these men will consent to live with us, to be one people, is if every male among us is circumcised, as they are circumcised.

23 מִקְנֵהֶם וְקִנְיָנָם וְכָל־בְּהֶמְתָּם הֲלוֹא לָנוּ הֵם אַךְ נֵאוֹתָה
לָהֶם וְיֵשְׁבוּ אִתָּנוּ:

23. Shall not their cattle and their wealth and every beast of theirs be ours? We only need to consent to them, and they will live with us."

24 וַיִּשְׁמְעוּ אֶל־חֲמוֹר וְאֶל־שְׁכֶם בְּנוֹ כָּל־יֹצְאֵי שַׁעַר עִירוֹ וַיִּמֹּלוּ
כָּל־זָכָר כָּל־יֹצְאֵי שַׁעַר עִירוֹ:

24. All of the men who went out from the gate of the city heeded Hamor and his son Shechem, and every male was circumcised.

What happened between Shechem and Dinah is unclear. Did Shechem violently force himself on a helpless and resisting Dinah, or was their sexual union consensual? Some commentators have taken Shechem's obvious love for Dinah and his subsequent willingness to make such a stunning sacrifice for her to be indications of the latter. If so, this becomes a case of statutory rape. Statutory rape is consensual sexual activity that is considered rape by statute, by custom, or by law, as when an adult engages in sex with someone who is under the age of consent. It is also possible that this is a case of "date rape" in which a seemingly friendly encounter is distorted into violent rape by the unwillingness of the male to "take no for an answer."

Which of the interpretations above strikes you as being correct?

Now read the rest of the chapter and see if your answer influences your reaction to what comes next.

Genesis 34:25–31

25 וַיְהִי בַיּוֹם הַשְּׁלִישִׁי בִּהְיוֹתָם כֹּאֲבִים וַיִּקְחוּ שְׁנֵי־בְנֵי־יַעֲקֹב
שִׁמְעוֹן וְלֵוִי אֲחֵי דִינָה אִישׁ חַרְבּוֹ וַיָּבֹאוּ עַל־הָעִיר בֶּטַח וַיַּהַרְגוּ
כָּל־זָכָר:

34:25. And it came to pass on the third day, when the men
were all still sore, that two of the sons of Jacob, Simeon
and Levi, Dinah's brothers, took up their swords and
came boldly upon the city, and they slew all of the males.

26 וְאֶת־חֲמוֹר וְאֶת־שְׁכֶם בְּנוֹ הָרְגוּ לְפִי־חָרֶב וַיִּקְחוּ אֶת־דִּינָה
מִבֵּית שְׁכֶם וַיֵּצֵאוּ:

26. They killed Hamor and his son Shechem with the edge
of the sword, and took Dinah out of Shechem's house,
and fled.

27 בְּנֵי יַעֲקֹב בָּאוּ עַל־הַחֲלָלִים וַיָּבֹזּוּ הָעִיר אֲשֶׁר טִמְּאוּ
אֲחוֹתָם:

27. The other sons of Jacob fell upon the slain city and
plundered it, because their sister had been defiled.

28 אֶת־צֹאנָם וְאֶת־בְּקָרָם וְאֶת־חֲמֹרֵיהֶם וְאֵת אֲשֶׁר־בָּעִיר
וְאֶת־אֲשֶׁר בַּשָּׂדֶה לָקָחוּ:

28. They took their sheep, and their oxen, and their asses,
and that which was in the city, and that which was in the
field,

29 וְאֶת־כָּל־חֵילָם וְאֶת־כָּל־טַפָּם וְאֶת־נְשֵׁיהֶם שָׁבוּ וַיָּבֹזּוּ וְאֵת
כָּל־אֲשֶׁר בַּבָּיִת:

29. And they carried off all their wealth, and all their
children, and their wives, and all that was in their homes.

45

30 וַיֹּאמֶר יַעֲקֹב אֶל־שִׁמְעוֹן וְאֶל־לֵוִי עֲכַרְתֶּם אֹתִי לְהַבְאִישֵׁנִי בְּיֹשֵׁב הָאָרֶץ בַּכְּנַעֲנִי וּבַפְּרִזִּי וַאֲנִי מְתֵי מִסְפָּר וְנֶאֶסְפוּ עָלַי וְהִכּוּנִי וְנִשְׁמַדְתִּי אֲנִי וּבֵיתִי:

30. And Jacob admonished Simeon and Levi, saying, "You have brought trouble on me, rendering me odious among the inhabitants of the land, among the Canaanites and the Perizzites. And, since we are few in number, they shall gather together against me and kill me, and I shall be destroyed, I and my household."

31 וַיֹּאמְרוּ הַכְזוֹנָה יַעֲשֶׂה אֶת־אֲחוֹתֵנוּ:

31. To which they responded, "So, should we have allowed him to deal with our sister as with a harlot?"

Imagine that you are the defense lawyer for the brothers of Dinah. What arguments would you use to defend their actions?

Imagine that you are the prosecutor. What arguments would you use to convict them?

Imagine that you are Dinah. Tell the story from your perspective.

7. Between Husband and Wife

At the conclusion of a Jewish wedding ceremony, the bride and groom enter a room alone together. This custom is known as יִחוּד (yichud), or "unity," and symbolizes the fact that from that time onward the bride and groom matter first to each other. In Judaism, the marital relationship is sacred and primary, as we see in the texts below.

Genesis 2:24

24 עַל־כֵּן יַעֲזָב־אִישׁ אֶת־אָבִיו וְאֶת־אִמּוֹ וְדָבַק בְּאִשְׁתּוֹ וְהָיוּ לְבָשָׂר אֶחָד:

2:24. Thus a man leaves his father and his mother and clings to his wife, so that they become one flesh.

This point is made even more strongly in the following midrashim.

Pirkei D'Rabbi Eliezer

Written in the eighth century, *Pirkei D'Rabbi Eliezer* is not strictly a book of midrashim. It begins, in fact, with an *aggadah*, or rabbinic story, about the life of Eliezer ben Hyrcanus, hence its name. It does include, however, midrashim dealing with biblical events from Creation through the story of the Exodus. It is not merely a collection of previously written stories, but rather a unified narrative in which the personality and perspective of the author comes through quite clearly.

Pirkei D'Rabbi Eliezer 32:2

שלש שנים עשה יצחק אבל על שרה אמו לאחר ג׳ שנים
לקח את רבקה ושכח אבל אמו מכאן אתה למד עד שלא
לקח אדם אשה אהבתו הולכת אחר הוריו לקח אשה
אהבתו הולכת אחר אשתו.

Isaac mourned his mother Sarah for three years. At the
end of three years, he married Rebekah and ceased to
mourn for his mother. Thus we see that up until the time
that a man takes a wife, his love is directed toward his
parents. Once he marries, however, he should direct his
love toward his wife.

Sefer Chasidim

Sefer Chasidim, or the *Book of the Pious*, was
written in large part by Rabbi Judah the Pious. It is
an ethical work, reflecting the teachings of
Ashkenazi Chasidim in twelfth- and early
thirteenth-century Germany. The book is intended
to instruct the pious how to act in everyday life:
how to dress, speak, pray, work, pick a wife,
conduct one's business, choose a teacher, and even
sleep. As a result, it became the basis for all of the
other Ashkenazi legal and ethical works that
succeeded it.

Sefer Chasidim, Section 952

ואם אביו או אמו בעלי קטטה ויש לו אשה ויודע שעל חנם
מתקוטטי׳ והדין עם אשתו לא יתכן לכעוס על אשתו כדי
לעשות נחת רוח לאביו ולאמו.

If your parents are always quarreling with your wife, and
you know that your wife is in the right, you should not
rebuke your wife in order to placate your parents.

There is, however, a problem here. Whatever happened to the Fifth Commandment? Is it simply abrogated after marriage?

Exodus 20:12

> 12 כַּבֵּד אֶת־אָבִיךָ וְאֶת־אִמֶּךָ לְמַעַן יַאֲרִכוּן יָמֶיךָ עַל הָאֲדָמָה אֲשֶׁר־יְהוָֹה אֱלֹהֶיךָ נֹתֵן לָךְ:

20:12. Honor your father and your mother that you may long endure on the land that *Adonai*, your God, is giving to you.

Why do you think the Rabbis made the decision to place the marital bond above even the parental bond? Do you think it is a healthy decision? What would you have decided?

What does this decision say about the nature of Jewish families?

8. Thou Shalt Not Commit Adultery

There is, of course, one commandment that does deal specifically with marriage.

Exodus 20:13

13 לֹא תִּנְאָף:

20:13. You shall not commit adultery.

Have you ever wanted something that someone else had? What did you do about it?

When one covets another person's spouse, the issues become even more complex. If those people are married, and if they act on their mutual attraction, it is known as adultery.

Second Samuel

After the Torah, we find the section of the Bible known as the Prophets, or נְבִיאִים (*N'vi-im*). The haftarot that we read on Shabbat are drawn largely from this section of the Bible. The prophets had a special and direct connection to God and therefore often served as voices of conscience to the people of Israel and to their kings. This text is drawn from the Book of Second Samuel, but focuses on a prophet known as Nathan.

II Samuel 11:2–6

2 וַיְהִי לְעֵת הָעֶרֶב וַיָּקָם דָּוִד מֵעַל מִשְׁכָּבוֹ וַיִּתְהַלֵּךְ עַל־גַּג בֵּית־
הַמֶּלֶךְ וַיַּרְא אִשָּׁה רֹחֶצֶת מֵעַל הַגָּג וְהָאִשָּׁה טוֹבַת מַרְאֶה
מְאֹד:

11:2. And it came to pass one evening that David arose
from his bed and walked on the roof of the royal palace,
and from the roof he saw a woman bathing herself. The
woman was very beautiful to look upon.

3 וַיִּשְׁלַח דָּוִד וַיִּדְרֹשׁ לָאִשָּׁה וַיֹּאמֶר הֲלוֹא־זֹאת בַּת־שֶׁבַע
בַּת־אֱלִיעָם אֵשֶׁת אוּרִיָּה הַחִתִּי:

3. David sent and inquired after the woman. And he said,
"Is this not Bathsheba, the daughter of Eliam, the wife of
Uriah the Hittite?"

4 וַיִּשְׁלַח דָּוִד מַלְאָכִים וַיִּקָּחֶהָ וַתָּבוֹא אֵלָיו וַיִּשְׁכַּב עִמָּהּ וְהִיא
מִתְקַדֶּשֶׁת מִטֻּמְאָתָהּ וַתָּשָׁב אֶל־בֵּיתָהּ:

4. And David sent messengers, who took her, and she
came in to him, and he lay with her, for she was purified
from her uncleanness. And she returned to her house.

5 וַתַּהַר הָאִשָּׁה וַתִּשְׁלַח וַתַּגֵּד לְדָוִד וַתֹּאמֶר הָרָה אָנֹכִי:

5. But the woman conceived, and she sent word to David,
saying, "I am with child."

6 וַיִּשְׁלַח דָּוִד אֶל־יוֹאָב שְׁלַח אֵלַי אֶת־אוּרִיָּה הַחִתִּי וַיִּשְׁלַח
יוֹאָב אֶת־אוּרִיָּה אֶל־דָּוִד:

6. And David sent to Yoav, saying, "Send me Uriah the
Hittite." And Joab sent Uriah to David.

King David has now gotten Uriah's wife pregnant. Uriah is one of David's key military officers. What options does David have at this point? What do you think he should do? What do you think he is going to do?

Kings are not immune from temptation. David, the king, has committed quite a serious offense. He has violated one of God's most sacred commandments. In the next passage, however, he greatly compounds his sin.

II Samuel 11:13

13 וַיִּקְרָא־לוֹ דָוִד וַיֹּאכַל לְפָנָיו וַיֵּשְׁתְּ וַיְשַׁכְּרֵהוּ וַיֵּצֵא בָעֶרֶב לִשְׁכַּב בְּמִשְׁכָּבוֹ עִם־עַבְדֵי אֲדֹנָיו וְאֶל־בֵּיתוֹ לֹא יָרָד:

11:13. David summoned Uriah, and he ate and drank with him, and he made him drunk. And in the evening, Uriah went out to lie on his bed with his lord's officers; he did not go down to his own house.

This is a key turning point in the story. David gets Uriah drunk and then expects that Uriah will go to spend the night with his wife Bathsheba.

If Uriah had indeed visited Bathsheba, would it have solved David's dilemma? How?

But alas, Uriah is a disciplined and dedicated officer, choosing instead to spend the night before battle with his soldiers. Paradoxically, it is this selfless act of duty in the service of his king that seals his fate.

II Samuel 11:14–17

14 וַיְהִי בַבֹּקֶר וַיִּכְתֹּב דָוִד סֵפֶר אֶל־יוֹאָב וַיִּשְׁלַח בְּיַד אוּרִיָּה:

11:14. And it came to pass in the morning that David wrote a letter to Joab and sent it by the hand of Uriah.

15 וַיִּכְתֹּב בַּסֵּפֶר לֵאמֹר הָבוּ אֶת־אוּרִיָּה אֶל־מוּל פְּנֵי הַמִּלְחָמָה הַחֲזָקָה וְשַׁבְתֶּם מֵאַחֲרָיו וְנִכָּה וָמֵת:

15. In the letter, he wrote, "Set Uriah in the front of the fiercest battle, and retire from him, that he may be struck and die."

16 וַיְהִי בִּשְׁמוֹר יוֹאָב אֶל־הָעִיר וַיִּתֵּן אֶת־אוּרִיָּה אֶל־הַמָּקוֹם אֲשֶׁר יָדַע כִּי אַנְשֵׁי־חַיִל שָׁם:

16. And it came to pass, when Joab observed the city, that he assigned Uriah to a place where he knew that the most dangerous enemy forces would be.

17 וַיֵּצְאוּ אַנְשֵׁי הָעִיר וַיִּלָּחֲמוּ אֶת־יוֹאָב וַיִּפֹּל מִן־הָעָם מֵעַבְדֵי דָוִד וַיָּמָת גַּם אוּרִיָּה הַחִתִּי:

17. And the men of the city went out, and fought with Joab, and some of David's officers fell, and Uriah the Hittite was among them.

In most societies, a king could get away with such a crime, but not in Israel. The kings of Israel answered to a "higher authority." The prophets were often the messengers of God's disapproval. Nathan was just such a prophet.

II Samuel 12:1–7

1 וַיִּשְׁלַח יְהֹוָה אֶת־נָתָן אֶל־דָּוִד וַיָּבֹא אֵלָיו וַיֹּאמֶר לוֹ שְׁנֵי אֲנָשִׁים הָיוּ בְּעִיר אֶחָת אֶחָד עָשִׁיר וְאֶחָד רָאשׁ:

12:1. And *Adonai* sent Nathan to David. And Nathan came before David and said, "There were two men in one city, the one rich, and the other poor.

2 לְעָשִׁיר הָיָה צֹאן וּבָקָר הַרְבֵּה מְאֹד׃

2. The rich man had very many flocks and herds.

3 וְלָרָשׁ אֵין־כֹּל כִּי אִם־כִּבְשָׂה אַחַת קְטַנָּה אֲשֶׁר קָנָה וַיְחַיֶּהָ
וַתִּגְדַּל עִמּוֹ וְעִם־בָּנָיו יַחְדָּו מִפִּתּוֹ תֹאכַל וּמִכֹּסוֹ תִשְׁתֶּה
וּבְחֵיקוֹ תִשְׁכָּב וַתְּהִי־לוֹ כְּבַת׃

3. But the poor man had nothing, save one little ewe lamb,
which he had bought and raised up. And it grew up
together with him and with his children. It ate of his own
food, and drank of his own cup, and lay in his bosom, and
was to him as a child.

4 וַיָּבֹא הֵלֶךְ לְאִישׁ הֶעָשִׁיר וַיַּחְמֹל לָקַחַת מִצֹּאנוֹ וּמִבְּקָרוֹ
לַעֲשׂוֹת לָאֹרֵחַ הַבָּא־לוֹ וַיִּקַּח אֶת־כִּבְשַׂת הָאִישׁ הָרָאשׁ וַיַּעֲשֶׂהָ
לָאִישׁ הַבָּא אֵלָיו׃

4. And there came a traveler to the rich man, but he was
unwilling to take from his own flock and of his own herd
to prepare a meal for the traveler who came to him, so he
took the poor man's lamb and prepared it for the man
who came to him."

5 וַיִּחַר־אַף דָּוִד בָּאִישׁ מְאֹד וַיֹּאמֶר אֶל־נָתָן חַי־יְהוָה כִּי
בֶן־מָוֶת הָאִישׁ הָעֹשֶׂה זֹאת׃

5. And David's anger was greatly kindled against the man,
and he said to Nathan, "As *Adonai* lives, the man who has
done this thing shall surely die.

6 וְאֶת־הַכִּבְשָׂה יְשַׁלֵּם אַרְבַּעְתָּיִם עֵקֶב אֲשֶׁר עָשָׂה אֶת־הַדָּבָר
הַזֶּה וְעַל אֲשֶׁר לֹא־חָמָל׃

6. And he shall restore the lamb fourfold, because he did
this thing, and because he had no pity."

‫7 וַיֹּאמֶר נָתָן אֶל־דָּוִד אַתָּה הָאִישׁ.‬

7. And Nathan said to David, "You are the man!"

What is the analogy that Nathan is making? Whom does the lamb represent? Who is the poor man? Which character in Nathan's parable represents David?

As a result of his sin, David is never allowed to build the Holy Temple in Jerusalem. That honor goes instead to his son, King Solomon.

The case of King David and Bathsheba is a clear case of adultery, and the consequences are quite clear as well. In real life, however, what constitutes adultery is not always so clear. Consider the following verse from the Talmud.

Talmud, *N'darim* 20b

‫מכאן אמר רבי: אל ישתה אדם בכוס זה ויתן עיניו בכוס‬
‫אחר.‬

Rabbi taught, one may not drink out of one goblet and think of another.

What is the meaning of this verse?

Would "drinking out of one goblet while thinking of another" constitute adultery in your relationships? Why or why not?

9. The Song of Songs

As you have probably already gathered, the Bible can be quite sexually explicit. Nowhere is this clearer than in the biblical book known as שִׁיר הַשִּׁירִים (Shir HaShirim), or the Song of Songs.

Song of Songs

The third section of the Bible is known as כְּתוּבִים (K'tuvim), or Writings. It is in this section that we find the Song of Songs, a book comprised entirely of love poetry. According to tradition, these poems were composed by the same King Solomon who built the Holy Temple. We read this beautiful book of love at the spring festival of Passover.

Song of Songs 1:1–4

1 שִׁיר הַשִּׁירִים אֲשֶׁר לִשְׁלֹמֹה:

1:1. The song of songs, which is Solomon's.

2 יִשָּׁקֵנִי מִנְּשִׁיקוֹת פִּיהוּ
כִּי־טוֹבִים דֹּדֶיךָ מִיָּיִן:

2. Let him kiss me with the kisses of his mouth, for your love is better than wine.

3 לְרֵיחַ שְׁמָנֶיךָ טוֹבִים
שֶׁמֶן תּוּרַק שְׁמֶךָ
עַל־כֵּן עֲלָמוֹת אֲהֵבוּךָ:

3. Your anointing oils are fragrant, your name is oil poured out. Therefore the maidens love you.

4 מָשְׁכֵנִי אַחֲרֶיךָ נָּרוּצָה
הֱבִיאַנִי הַמֶּלֶךְ חֲדָרָיו
נָגִילָה וְנִשְׂמְחָה בָּךְ
נַזְכִּירָה דֹדֶיךָ
מִיַּיִן מֵישָׁרִים אֲהֵבוּךָ:

4. Draw me after you and we will run. The king has brought me into his chambers. We will be glad and rejoice in you. We will praise your love more than wine; rightly they love you.

At first blush, what do you think this poem is about? Does it surprise you that it is found in the Bible?

Some of the love images in this poem are familiar to us; some seem strange to our ears.

Song of Songs 1:9–11

9 לְסֻסָתִי בְּרִכְבֵי פַרְעֹה דִּמִּיתִיךְ רַעְיָתִי:

1:9. I compare you, O my love, to a mare of the chariots of Pharaoh.

10 נָאווּ לְחָיַיִךְ בַּתֹּרִים צַוָּארֵךְ בַּחֲרוּזִים:

10. Your cheeks are comely with rows of jewels, your neck with strings of beads.

57

11 תּוֹרֵי זָהָב נַעֲשֶׂה־לָּךְ עִם נְקֻדּוֹת הַכָּסֶף׃

11. We will make you ornaments of gold studded with silver.

If we were writing a love poem, we might say that someone is as beautiful as a flower. What images of beauty are being used here?

How would your boyfriend or girlfriend react to being compared to a horse? What does that say about the nature of beauty? About the nature of poetry? About the differences in our respective societies?

Nature, in general, plays an important role in the love imagery.

Song of Songs 1:12–17

12 עַד־שֶׁהַמֶּלֶךְ בִּמְסִבּוֹ נִרְדִּי נָתַן רֵיחוֹ׃

1:12. While the king was reclining at his table, my perfume sent forth its fragrance.

13 צְרוֹר הַמֹּר דּוֹדִי לִי בֵּין שָׁדַי יָלִין׃

13. My beloved is to me a bundle of myrrh that lies between my breasts.

14 אֶשְׁכֹּל הַכֹּפֶר דּוֹדִי לִי בְּכַרְמֵי עֵין גֶּדִי׃

14. My beloved is to me a cluster of henna in the vineyards of En-Gedi.

15 הִנָּךְ יָפָה רַעְיָתִי הִנָּךְ יָפָה עֵינַיִךְ יוֹנִים׃

15. Behold, you are beautiful, my love. Behold, you are beautiful. Your eyes are like doves.

16 הִנְּךָ יָפֶה דוֹדִי אַף נָעִים אַף־עַרְשֵׂנוּ רַעֲנָנָה:

16. Behold, you are beautiful, my beloved, truly lovely. Our couch is green.

17 קֹרוֹת בָּתֵּינוּ אֲרָזִים רַהִיטֵנוּ בְּרוֹתִים:

17. The beams of our house are cedar, and our rafters are of cypress.

What does this last line mean? Where are the lovers lying?

What metaphors are being used here? Why? How effective are they in conveying the feelings of the author?

The sexual imagery often becomes quite explicit. If this poem were not in the Bible, it would probably be banned from our classrooms.

Song of Songs 2:1–17

1 אֲנִי חֲבַצֶּלֶת הַשָּׁרוֹן שׁוֹשַׁנַּת הָעֲמָקִים:

2:1. I am the rose of Sharon, a lily of the valleys.

2 כְּשׁוֹשַׁנָּה בֵּין הַחוֹחִים כֵּן רַעְיָתִי בֵּין הַבָּנוֹת:

2. Like a lily among thorns, so is my love among the maidens.

3 כְּתַפּוּחַ בַּעֲצֵי הַיַּעַר כֵּן דּוֹדִי בֵּין הַבָּנִים בְּצִלּוֹ חִמַּדְתִּי וְיָשַׁבְתִּי וּפִרְיוֹ מָתוֹק לְחִכִּי:

3. Like the apple tree among the trees of the wood, so is my beloved among young men. I sat down under his shadow with great delight, and his fruit was sweet to my taste.

4 הֱבִיאַנִי אֶל־בֵּית הַיָּיִן וְדִגְלוֹ עָלַי אַהֲבָה:

4. He brought me to the banqueting house, and his banner over me was love.

5 סַמְּכוּנִי בָּאֲשִׁישׁוֹת רַפְּדוּנִי בַּתַּפּוּחִים כִּי־חוֹלַת אַהֲבָה אָנִי:

5. Sustain me with raisins, comfort me with apples, for I am sick with love.

6 שְׂמֹאלוֹ תַּחַת לְרֹאשִׁי וִימִינוֹ תְּחַבְּקֵנִי:

6. His left hand is under my head, and his right hand embraces me.

7 הִשְׁבַּעְתִּי אֶתְכֶם בְּנוֹת יְרוּשָׁלַם בִּצְבָאוֹת אוֹ בְּאַיְלוֹת הַשָּׂדֶה אִם־תָּעִירוּ וְאִם־תְּעוֹרְרוּ אֶת־הָאַהֲבָה עַד שֶׁתֶּחְפָּץ:

7. I adjure you, O daughters of Jerusalem, by the gazelles or by the hinds of the field, that you stir not up, nor awake my love, until it please.

8 קוֹל דּוֹדִי הִנֵּה־זֶה בָּא מְדַלֵּג עַל־הֶהָרִים מְקַפֵּץ עַל־הַגְּבָעוֹת:

8. The voice of my beloved! Behold, he comes leaping upon the mountains, skipping upon the hills.

9 דּוֹמֶה דוֹדִי לִצְבִי אוֹ לְעֹפֶר הָאַיָּלִים הִנֵּה־זֶה עוֹמֵד אַחַר כָּתְלֵנוּ מַשְׁגִּיחַ מִן־הַחַלֹּנוֹת מֵצִיץ מִן־הַחֲרַכִּים:

9. My beloved is like a gazelle or a young deer. Behold, he stands behind our wall, gazing in at the windows, looking through the lattice.

10 עָנָה דוֹדִי וְאָמַר לִי קוּמִי לָךְ רַעְיָתִי יָפָתִי וּלְכִי־לָךְ:

10. My beloved speaks and says to me, "Arise, my love, my fair one, and come away.

11 כִּי־הִנֵּה הַסְּתָיו עָבָר הַגֶּשֶׁם חָלַף הָלַךְ לוֹ:

11. For, lo, the winter is past, the rain is over and gone;

12 הַנִּצָּנִים נִרְאוּ בָאָרֶץ עֵת הַזָּמִיר הִגִּיעַ וְקוֹל הַתּוֹר נִשְׁמַע בְּאַרְצֵנוּ:

12. The flowers appear on the earth; the time of the songbird has come, and the voice of the turtledove is heard in our land.

13 הַתְּאֵנָה חָנְטָה פַגֶּיהָ וְהַגְּפָנִים סְמָדַר נָתְנוּ רֵיחַ קוּמִי לָךְ רַעְיָתִי יָפָתִי וּלְכִי־לָךְ:

13. The fig tree puts forth her green figs, and the vines in blossom give forth their scent. Arise, my love, my fair one, and come away.

14 יוֹנָתִי בְּחַגְוֵי הַסֶּלַע בְּסֵתֶר הַמַּדְרֵגָה הַרְאִינִי אֶת־מַרְאַיִךְ הַשְׁמִיעִינִי אֶת־קוֹלֵךְ כִּי־קוֹלֵךְ עָרֵב וּמַרְאֵיךְ נָאוֶה:

14. O my dove, in the clefts of the rock, in the secret places of the cliff, let me see your face, let me hear your voice, for your voice is sweet, and your face is beautiful."

15 אֶחֱזוּ־לָנוּ שׁוּעָלִים שׁוּעָלִים קְטַנִּים מְחַבְּלִים כְּרָמִים וּכְרָמֵינוּ סְמָדַר:

15. Catch for us the foxes, the little foxes that spoil the vineyards, for our vineyards are in blossom.

16 דּוֹדִי לִי וַאֲנִי לוֹ הָרֹעֶה בַּשׁוֹשַׁנִּים:

16. My beloved is mine, and I am his. He pastures his flock among the lilies.

17 עַד שֶׁיָּפוּחַ הַיּוֹם וְנָסוּ הַצְּלָלִים סֹב דְּמֵה־לְךָ דוֹדִי לִצְבִי אוֹ
לְעֹפֶר הָאַיָּלִים עַל־הָרֵי בָתֶר:

17. Until the day cools, and the shadows flee away, turn, my beloved, and be like a gazelle or a young deer upon the mountains of spices.

Why do you think this very sexy book was included in the Bible?

This is obviously a love poem, but who is writing to whom? A man to a woman? A woman to a man? A man to a man? A woman to a woman?

The traditional answer to this quandary is very clear. The Rabbis did not see this as a love poem between two people at all; rather they read it as a love poem between God and the People of Israel. Go back and reread the above texts in this light.

How does this change your understanding of these verses?

10. Sexual Pleasure

We often think of religious authorities as prudish, striving to repress all sexual enjoyment. Such is not always the case in Judaism, however, as we shall see in the texts that follow.

Talmud, *K'tubot* 61b

העונה האמורה בתורה, הטיילין — בכל יום, הפועלים — שתים בשבת, החמרים — אחת בשבת, הגמלים — אחת לשלשים יום, הספנים — אחת לששה חדשים.

> The times for conjugal duty prescribed in the Torah are: for men of independent means, every day; for laborers, twice a week; for donkey drivers, once a week; for camel drivers, once in thirty days; for sailors, once in six months.

So we see that sexual pleasure is a wife's right and a husband's obligation.

But why is this obligation different for a laborer than it is for a sailor?

Why then is the marital obligation less for a camel driver than for a donkey driver?

Isn't it interesting that the woman's rights to sexual pleasure are clearly spelled out? This is especially remarkable in light of the following text.

Talmud, *Eiruvin* 100b

> אסור לאדם שיכוף אשתו לדבר מצוה,... ואמר רבי יהושע
> בן לוי: כל הכופה אשתו לדבר מצוה הויין לו בנים שאינן
> מהוגנין.

> A man is forbidden to compel his wife to have marital
> relations.... Rabbi Joshua ben Levi similarly stated:
> Whosoever compels his wife to have marital relations will
> have unworthy children.

So a man may not compel his wife to fulfill the marital obligation. And
yet a wife seems to have the right to compel her husband. It is thus the
husband's obligation to ensure that his wife is sexually fulfilled.

Talmud, *Y'vamot* 62b

> אמר ריב"ל: כל היודע באשתו שהיא יראת שמים ואינו
> פוקדה — נקרא חוטא.

> Rabbi Joshua ben Levi said, "Whosoever knows his wife
> to be a God-fearing woman and does not duly visit her is
> called a sinner."

Of course, it could be argued that the above texts are concerned only
with a woman's right to procreation. In the following texts, however,
it is clear that it is the sharing of sexual pleasure that is a husband's
obligation to his wife.

Talmud, *Eiruvin* 100b

> אמר רבי יוחנן אילמלא לא ניתנה תורה היינו למידין
> צניעות מחתול וגזל מנמלה ועריות מיונה דרך ארץ
> מתרנגול שמפייס ואחר כך בועל ומאי מפייס לה אמר רב

יהודה אמר רב הכי קאמר לה זבינא ליך זיגא דמטו ליך עד
כרעיך לבתר הכי אמר לה לישמטתיה לכרבלתיה דההוא
תרנגולא אי אית ליה ולא זביננא ליך.

Rabbi Yochanan observed: "If the Torah had not been
given, we could have learned modesty from the cat,
honesty from the ant, chastity from the dove, and good
manners from the rooster, who first coaxes and then
mates."

Talmud, *K'tubot* 48a

שארה זו קרוב בשר שלא ינהג בה מנהג פרסיים שמשמשין
מטותיהן בלבושיהן מסייע ליה לרב הונא דאמר רב הונא
האומר אי אפשי אלא אני בבגדי והיא בבגדה יוציא ונותן
כתובה.

There must be close bodily contact during sex. This means
that a husband must not treat his wife in the manner of
the Persians, who perform their marital duties in their
clothes. This provides support for the ruling of Rav Huna,
who ruled that a husband who says, "I will not perform
my marital duties unless she wears her clothes and
I mine," must divorce her and give her also her *ketubah*
settlement.

In other words, if a husband refuses to perform his marital obligation in
a loving, romantic, and sexually pleasing way, his wife actually has the
right to demand a divorce and to receive her *ketubah* settlement.
Since divorce was generally considered to be a husband's prerogative,
this is a remarkable statement about the importance of sexual pleasure
within a marriage.

We generally think of traditional Judaism as being concerned only with procreation. What do these texts teach us about Judaism's view of sex within marriage?

In his *Mishneh Torah*, Maimonides takes an even more remarkably progressive view of sexual pleasure.

Mishneh Torah

The *Mishneh Torah* was composed by Moses Maimonides (1135–1204). Because his Hebrew name was **Rabbi Moses ben Maimon**, he was also known as the **Rambam**. Maimonides was the most significant Jewish philosopher of the Middle Ages. Through his work on the *Mishneh Torah*, a commentary on the Mishnah, Maimonides came to be recognized as the preeminent rabbinic codifier of Jewish law. In this seminal legal work, he was able to organize the disparate rulings of the Talmud into clearly organized chapters, providing his own rulings at the conclusion of each.

Mishneh Torah, Laws Concerning Forbidden Relations 21:9

אשתו של אדם מותרת היא לו. לפיכך כל מה שאדם רוצה
לעשות באשתו עושה. בועל בכל עת שירצה ומנשק בכל
אבר ואבר שירצה. ובא עליה כדרכה ושלא כדרכה ובלבד
שלא יוציא שכבת זרע לבטלה ואע״פ כן מדת חסידות שלא
יקל אדם את ראשו לכך ושיקדש עצמו בשעת תשמיש.

Since a man's wife is permitted to him, he may act with her in any manner whatsoever. He may have intercourse with her whenever he so desires and kiss any organ of her body he wishes, and he may have intercourse with her naturally or unnaturally, provided that he does not expend semen to no purpose. Nevertheless, it is an attribute of piety that a man should not act in this matter with levity and that he should sanctify himself at the time of intercourse.

Earlier we spoke about the Torah's first commandment. What was it, and how does it explain Maimonides' restriction against expending semen to no purpose?

What do you think the Rambam might mean when he says that we must sanctify ourselves at the time of sexual relations?

What is the general attitude toward sexuality being expressed by the Rambam? Given that this was written by a rabbi in the Middle Ages, is this a surprise?

The above texts are remarkably progressive; they sound as if they could have been written today. This is not to say, however, that the Rabbis were totally liberated. Consider the following texts.

Talmud, *Nidah* 17a

אמר רב חסדא אסור לו לאדם שישמש מטתו ביום שנאמר
ואהבת לרעך כמוך מאי משמע אמר אביי שמא יראה בה
דבר מגונה ותתגנה עליו.

Rav Chisda ruled: A man is forbidden to perform his marital duty in the daytime, for it is said, AND THOU SHALT LOVE THY NEIGHBOR AS THYSELF (Leviticus 19:18). But what is the proof? Abaye replied, "He might observe something repulsive in her, and she would thereby become loathsome to him."

Talmud, *Gittin* 70a

שלשה דברים מתיזין גופו של אדם ואלו הן אכל מעומד
ושתה מעומד ושימש מטתו מעומד.

Three things enfeeble a man's body, namely, to eat
standing, to drink standing, and to have marital
intercourse in a standing position.

Talmud, *Nidah* 13b

תנא דבי רבי ישמעאל לא תנאף לא תהא בך ניאוף בין ביד
בין ברגל.

It was taught at the school of Rabbi Ishmael, "Thou shall
not commit adultery" implies, Thou shall not practice
masturbation either with hand or with foot.

*What might explain the differences in attitude regarding sexuality that
we find in the traditional texts? Remember that these rabbinic texts
were all written down by human beings.*

11. Breaking Up Is Hard to Do

"Breaking up is hard to do." These words do not come from the Talmud... but they should have! The following words, however, do come from the Talmud and say very much the same thing.

Talmud, *Sanhedrin* 7a

כי רחימתין הוה עזיזא — אפותיא דספסירא שכיבן,
השתא דלא עזיזא רחימתין — פוריא בר שיתין גרמידי
לא סגי לן.

When love is strong, a bed thin as the edge of a blade is sufficient, but when love grows weak, a bed of sixty cubits is not large enough.

In Judaism, divorce is not a sin, but it is no blessing either. The Rabbis do not consider divorce a violation of God's laws, but as we will discover in the texts below, their perspective was that one's connection to one's first spouse can never be fully broken.

Talmud, *B'rachot* 32b

אדם נושא אשה על אשתו ראשונה זוכר מעשה הראשונה.

When a man takes a second wife after his first, he still remembers the deeds of the first.

Talmud, *P'sachim* 112a

דאמר מר גרוש שנשא גרושה ארבע דעות במטה.

A Master said, "When a divorced man marries a divorced woman, there are four minds in the bed."

What does the Master mean when he says that if two divorced people marry, there are four minds in the bed? What problems might this create for the new marriage?

In certain circumstances, divorce is even required, or at least encouraged. In cases where a couple does not produce a child within ten years, for instance, the husband may divorce his wife in order to find a wife with whom he can produce offspring. This totally ignores the fact that infertility can be a male as well as a female problem, but nevertheless this was the law. With this in mind, consider the following text.

Shir HaShirim Rabbah

Shir HaShirim Rabbah is a midrashic commentary on the Song of Songs that proceeds verse by verse. The date of its composition is unknown, although it is assumed that, like many other midrashic collections, it had its origins in the Jewish community of Palestine.

Shir HaShirim Rabbah 1:30

ד"א נגילה ונשמחה בך תמן תנינן נשא אדם אשה ושהה
עמה עשר שנים ולא ילדה אינו רשאי ליבטל אמר רבי אידי
מעשה באשה אחת בצידן ששהתה עשר שנים עם בעלה
ולא ילדה אתון גבי ר' שמעון בן יוחאי בעיין למשתבקא דין
מדין אמר להון חייכון כשם שנזדווגתם זה לזה במאכל

ובמשתה כך אין אתם מתפרשים אלא מתוך מאכל ומשתה
הלכו בדרכיו ועשו לעצמן י"ט ועשו סעודה גדולה ושכרתו
יותר מדאי כיון שנתיישבה דעתו עליו אמר לה בתי ראי כל
חפץ טוב שיש לי בבית וטלי אותו ולכי לבית אביך מה
עשתה היא לאחר שישן רמזה לעבדייה ולשפחותיה ואמרה
להם שאוהו במטה וקחו אותו והוליכוהו לבית אבא
בחצי הלילה ננער משנתיה כיון דפג חמריה אמר לה בתי
היכן אני נתון אמרה ליה בבית אבא אמר לה מה לי לבית
אביך אמרה ליה ולא כך אמרת לי בערב כל חפץ טוב שיש
בביתי טלי אותו ולכי לבית אביך אין חפץ טוב לי בעולם
יותר ממך.

Another explanation of, WE WILL BE GLAD AND REJOICE
IN YOU (Song of Songs 1:4). We have learned elsewhere
(*Y'vamot* 64a) that "if a man has married a wife and lived
with her ten years and she has not given him a child, he is
not at liberty to neglect the duty of fathering children
[and so may divorce her to marry someone else]." Rabbi Idi said,
"It happened once that a woman in Sidon had lived ten
years with her husband without bearing him a child. They
came to Rabbi Simeon ben Yochai and requested to be
divorced. He said to them, 'I urge you, just as you have
always shared festive meals together, so do not part
without some festivity.' They took his advice and
observed a holiday and made a great feast and drank
very freely. Being in a magnanimous frame of mind, he
said to her, 'My dear, pick out anything you want in my
house and take it with you to your father's house.' What
did she do? When he was asleep, she gave an order to her
servants and handmaids to lift him up on the bed and
carry him to her father's home. At midnight he awoke
from his sleep, and when the effect of the wine had passed,

he said, 'My dear, where am I?' She replied, 'You are in my father's house.' 'And what am I doing in your father's house?' he said. She replied, 'Did you not say to me last night, "Take anything you like from my house with you to your father's house"? There is nothing in the world I care for more than you.'"

Sometimes, it seems, love does overcome all and they do indeed live happily ever after.

12. Sexism in the Texts

As you read the following texts, which reflect what we would call sexism or male chauvinism, remember that they were written centuries ago and reflect the mores and sensibilities of an age that has long since passed.

Talmud, *N'darim* 20b

> כל מה שאדם רוצה לעשות באשתו עושה משל לבשר הבא
> מבית הטבח רצה לאכלו במלח אוכלו צלי אוכלו מבושל
> אוכלו שלוק אוכלו וכן דג הבא מבית הצייד.

A man may do whatever he pleases with his wife during sexual intercourse. A parable: meat that comes from the butcher may be eaten salted, roasted, cooked, or seethed; so it is with fish from the fishmonger.

At first this text might seem quite enlightened from a sexual point of view, in that it encourages couples to engage in experimentation. However, the parable implies a more sexist intent.

How so? What does the parable imply about the relationship between men and women?

Talmud, *Kiddushin* 2b

מה אמרה תורה כי יקח איש אשה ולא כתב כי תלקח אשה
לאיש מפני שדרכו של איש לחזר על אשה ואין דרכה של
אשה לחזר על איש משל לאדם שאבדה לו אבידה מי חוזר
על מי בעל אבידה מחזר על אבידתו.

Why did the Torah state, IF ANY MAN TAKE A WIFE
(Deuteronomy 22:13), and not "If any woman take a
husband"? Because it is the way of a man to go in search
of a woman, but it is not the way of a woman to go in
search of a man. This may be compared to a man who lost
an article. Who goes in search of whom? The loser goes in
search of the lost article.

*If the Talmud had been written by women, how might this issue have
been addressed?*

*Ignoring for a moment the issue of the "lost article," what do you think
of the assertion of this text that it is the way of a man to go in search of
a woman but not the reverse? Can a woman ask a man out on a date?
Should she? Can a woman ask a man to marry her? Should she?*

*According to Martin Buber, would a relationship between a man and a
woman as described in the above text be considered I-Thou or I-It?
Why?*

Talmud, *Y'vamot* 63a

קפוץ זבין ארעא מתון נסיב איתתא נחית דרגא נסיב איתתא
סק דרגא בחר שושבינא.

Be quick in buying land. Be deliberate in taking a wife.
Come down a step in choosing your wife. Go up a step in
selecting your best man.

Why do you think the Talmud would advise a man to go down a step in choosing a wife, but up a step in selecting a best man? What is your reaction to this advice?

Talmud, *K'tubot* 65a

תנא: כוס אחד יפה לאשה, שנים — ניוול הוא, שלשה — תובעת בפה, ארבעה — אפילו תובעת חמור בשוק ואינה מקפדת. אמר רבא: לא שנו אלא שאין בעלה עמה, אבל בעלה עמה לית לן בה.

A *Tanna* taught, "One cup of wine is becoming to a woman; two are degrading. With three she solicits publicly. With four she solicits even a donkey in the street and does not care." Raba said, "This was taught only in respect of a woman whose husband is not with her, but if her husband is with her the objection to her drinking is nullified."

Ignoring the sexism of this text for just a moment, what is the Talmud telling us about the relationship between drinking and sexual promiscuity?

In this light, consider the following text.

Talmud, *Kiddushin* 2b

דדרכא דמיכלא יתירא לאתויי לידי זיבה, ודרכא דמישתיא יתירא לאתויי לידי זיבה.

It is the nature of excessive eating to cause gonorrhea, and it is the nature of excessive drinking to cause gonorrhea.

75

Why would the Rabbis believe that excessive eating and drinking might lead to the contracting of a sexually transmitted disease? Is there any truth to this?

What can we conclude then about the Rabbis' understanding of the relationship between alcohol and sexuality?

At times it appears that the Rabbis are simply afraid of the sexual allure of women.

Talmud, *B'rachot* 24a

א"ר יצחק טפח באשה ערוה למאי אילימא לאסתכולי בה
והא א"ר ששת למה מנה הכתוב תכשיטין שבחוץ עם
תכשיטין שבפנים לומר לך כל המסתכל באצבע קטנה של
אשה כאילו מסתכל במקום התורף אלא באשתו ולק"ש
אמר רב חסדא שוק באשה ערוה שנאמר גלי שוק עברי
נהרות וכתיב תגל ערותך וגם תראה חרפתך אמר שמואל
קול באשה ערוה שנא' כי קולך ערב ומראך נאוה אמר רב
ששת שער באשה ערוה שנא' שערך כעדר העזים.

Rav Isaac said, "A handbreadth of exposed flesh on a married woman constitutes sexual incitement." In which way? Should we say, if one gazes at it? But has not Rav Sheshet said, "Why does the Torah enumerate the ornaments worn outside the clothes as well as the undergarments (Numbers 31:50)? To tell you that if a man gazes at the little finger of a woman, it is as if he gazed at her secret place! Indeed this actually refers even to a man's own wife, during the time he is reciting the *Sh'ma*." Rav Chisda said, "A woman's leg is a sexual incitement, as it says, UNCOVER THE LEG, PASS THROUGH THE RIVERS (Isaiah 47:2) and then, YOUR NAKEDNESS SHALL BE UNCOVERED. INDEED YOUR SHAME SHALL BE

SEEN (Isaiah 47:3)." Samuel said, "A woman's voice is a sexual incitement, as it is written, FOR SWEET IS YOUR VOICE AND YOUR FACE IS BEAUTIFUL (Song of Songs 2:14)." Rav Sheshet said, "A woman's hair is a sexual incitement, as it says, YOUR HAIR IS AS A FLOCK OF GOATS (Song of Songs 4:1)."

This is a key text in terms of a woman's role within a traditional Jewish context.

If gazing at the little finger of a woman is the same as gazing at her genitals, and if looking upon a woman's hair is paramount to sexual incitement, what implications would this have for the standard of dress? For friendships between men and women? For the role of women in society?

The fact that a woman's voice (קוֹל אִשָּׁה, *kol ishah*) was also considered a sexual incitement had a chilling effect on the role of women within the life of the synagogue.

Explain why this would be the case.

Do you find that these restrictions are still prevalent in the society in which you live? In your synagogue? Why or why not?

Talmud, *Avodah Zarah* 25b

אשה כלי זיינה עליה.

A woman's weapons are upon her.

What does this mean?

Why does the text not say a man's weapons are upon him? What does this say about the way men sometimes view women? How do you feel about this stereotype?

Sometimes, however, the Rabbis reveal a remarkable sensitivity toward women. As we shall see, the texts are not always sexist.

Talmud, *Eiruvin* 100b

האשה תובעת בלב והאיש תובע בפה והיא מדה טובה בנשים.

A woman woos with her heart, while a man woos with his mouth. This is a superior trait in women.

What does this mean, and do you agree? Why or why not?

Talmud, *Nidah* 45b

שנתן הקב"ה בינה יתירה באשה יותר מבאיש.

The Holy One, blessed be, endowed the woman with more understanding than the man.

Do you agree? Why or why not?

Are the two texts above sexist as well? Why or why not?

Talmud, *Chulin* 84b

לעולם יאכל אדם וישתה — פחות ממה שיש לו, וילבש ויתכסה — במה שיש לו, ויכבד אשתו ובניו — יותר ממה שיש לו, שהן תלויין בו.

A man should always eat and drink less than his means allow, clothe himself in accordance with his means, and honor his wife and children more than his means allow, for they are dependent upon him.

What is your reaction to this text? Why? What does it say about the role of a Jewish husband?

B'reishit Rabbah 17:7

מעשה בחסיד אחד שהיה נשוי לחסידה אחת ולא העמידו
בנים זה מזה אמרו אין אנו מועילים להקב״ה כלום עמדו
וגרשו זה את זה הלך זה ונשא רשעה אחת ועשתה אותו
רשע הלכה זאת ונשאת לרשע אחד ועשתה אותו צדיק הוי
שהכל מן האשה.

It once happened that a pious man was married to a pious
woman, but they did not produce children. They
lamented, "We are of no use to the Holy One, blessed
be," and so they decided to get a divorce. The husband
went out and married a wicked woman, and she made him
wicked, while the wife went out and married a wicked
man, but she made him righteous. This proves that all
depends on the woman.

*What is your reaction to this text? Why? What does it say about the role
of a Jewish wife?*

13. Faulty Science in the Texts

As wise as they were, the Sages did not know everything. Nowhere is that seen more clearly than in the following texts.

Talmud, *Y'vamot* 34a

והא אין אשה מתעברת בביאה ראשונה.

Surely, no woman conceives from the first contact!

Talmud, *Sanhedrin* 37b

גמירי שאין האשה מתעברת מעומד.

We know by tradition that a woman cannot conceive in a standing position.

Sometimes the Sages were simply wrong from a scientific point of view. These texts illustrate that point dramatically! Obviously a woman can conceive from her first sexual intercourse and from intercourse performed in any position whatsoever.

Talmud, *B'rachot* 60a

היתה אשתו מעוברת ואמר יהיה רצון שתלד כו' הרי זו
תפלת שוא. ולא מהני רחמי? מתיב רב יוסף: (בראשית ל')
ואחר ילדה בת ותקרא את שמה דינה, מאי ואחר? אמר רב:
לאחר שדנה לאה דין בעצמה ואמרה: שנים עשר שבטים
עתידין לצאת מיעקב, ששה יצאו ממנו, וארבעה מן
השפחות — הרי עשרה, אם זה זכר — לא תהא אחותי

רחל כאחת השפחות! מיד נהפכה לבת, שנאמר ותקרא את
שמה דינה! — אין מזכירין מעשה נסים. ואיבעית אימא:
מעשה דלאה — בתוך ארבעים יום הוה. כדתניא: שלשה
ימים הראשונים — יבקש אדם רחמים שלא יסריח,
משלשה ועד ארבעים — יבקש רחמים שיהא זכר,
מארבעים יום ועד שלשה חדשים — יבקש רחמים שלא
יהא סנדל, משלשה חדשים ועד ששה — יבקש רחמים
שלא יהא נפל, מששה ועד תשעה — יבקש רחמים שיצא
בשלום. — ומי מהני רחמי? והאמר רב יצחק בריה דרב
אמי: איש מזריע תחלה — יולדת נקבה, אשה מזרעת
תחלה — יולדת זכר, שנאמר (ויקרא י״ב) אשה כי תזריע
וילדה זכר! — הכא במאי עסקינן — כגון שהזריעו שניהם
בבת אחת.

MISHNAH: If a man's wife is pregnant and he says,
"may God grant that my wife bear a son," this is a vain
prayer. GEMARA: Are such prayers then ineffectual?
Rav Joseph objected, citing the following: AND AFTER-
WARD SHE BORE A DAUGHTER AND CALLED HER NAME
DINAH (Genesis 30:21). What is meant by "afterward"? Rav
said, "After Leah had passed judgment on herself, saying,
'Twelve tribes are destined to issue from Jacob. Six have
issued from me, and four from the handmaids, making
ten. If this child will be a male, my sister Rachel will not
be equal to one of the handmaids.' Forthwith the child
was transformed into a girl, as it says, AND SHE CALLED
HER NAME DINAH [which means "judgment"]. We cannot,
however, cite a miraculous event in refuting a Mishnah.
Alternatively, I may reply that the incident of Leah
occurred within forty days after conception, according to
what has been taught: Within the first three days a man
should pray that the seed should not putrefy; from the

third to the fortieth day he should pray that the child should be a male; from the fortieth day to three months he should pray that it should not be a miscarriage; from three months to six months he should pray that it should not be stillborn; from six months to nine months he should pray for a safe delivery. But does such a prayer have an effect? Has not Rav Isaac the son of Rav Ammi said, "If the man orgasms first, the child will be a girl; if the woman orgasms first, the child will be a boy"? With what case are we dealing here? What if, for instance, they both have their orgasms at the same time.

This is a complicated text. The point of the Mishnah is that praying for a boy is an exercise in futility. In the Gemara, however, R. Joseph raises an objection. What about the midrash that claims that Leah miraculously changed the gender of her baby Dinah from a boy to a girl in the womb through prayer? Does this midrashic story not prove that prayers can affect the gender of the baby? The first objection to this presented by the Gemara is that a miracle cannot refute a Mishnah. The second is that Leah did indeed affect the gender of her baby through prayer, but that she was able to do so only because she prayed at the right time for such prayers in her gestational cycle. This, however, still leaves the original question, "but does such a prayer have an effect" whenever it is made? At this point the text defers to the saying of Rav Isaac the son of Rav Ammi, who believed that "if the man orgasms first, the child will be a girl," whereas "if the woman orgasms first, the child will be a boy." The Gemara takes this as scientific fact and therefore rules that such prayers only work in cases in which the male and female have had a simultaneous orgasm.

This may be good rabbinic logic, but it is most certainly faulty science!

Talmud, *Nidah* 31a

דתנן חבלי של נקבה מרובין משל זכר ואמר רבי אלעזר מאי
קרא אשר עשיתי בסתר רקמתי בתחתיות ארץ דרתי לא
נאמר אלא רקמתי מאי שנא חבלי נקבה מרובין משל זכר
זה בא כדרך תשמישו וזה בא כדרך תשמישו זו הופכת פניה
וזה אין הופך פניו.

Why are the pains of a female birth greater than those of a
male birth? The female emerges in the position she
assumes during intercourse and the male emerges in the
position he assumes during intercourse. The female,
therefore, turns her face upward [increasing the pain of
childbirth], while the male need not turn his face at all.

The Rabbis were brilliant and enlightening in so many areas. Biology,
however, was obviously not always their best subject.

14. But We're Only Human

Judaism believes that people are born with a pure soul. Sometimes, however, we give in to the יֵצֶר הָרָע (yetzer hara), to the evil inclination that is within us all. We are unable to resist the temptations that life places before us. We might expect a religious tradition to condemn such behavior in the strongest possible terms. In the text that follows, however, the Rabbis exhibit a remarkable and indeed a surprising amount of empathy for one who is compelled to sin.

Talmud, *Kiddushin* 40a

אם רואה אדם שיצר מתגבר עליו ילך למקום שאין מכירין
אותו וילבש שחורים ויתכסה שחורים ויעשה כמו שלבו
חפץ ואל יחלל שם שמים בפרהסיא.

If a man sees that his evil inclination is conquering him, let him go to a place where he is unknown, cloak himself with black, and do as his heart desires, but let him not publicly profane God's name [by sinning where he is known].

Why would the Rabbis have made such an exception to the laws of God? Why did they exhibit such surprising flexibility? What do you think of their decision to allow for this moral "release valve"?

Are there any dangers inherent in this kind of permissiveness? What are they?

Our sins, however, affect other people as well as ourselves. This is where the Rabbis draw the line, as is seen in the following text.

Talmud, *Sanhedrin* 75a

אמר רב יהודה אמר רב: מעשה באדם אחד שנתן עיניו
באשה אחת, והעלה לבו טינא. ובאו ושאלו לרופאים,
ואמרו: אין לו תקנה עד שתבעל. אמרו חכמים: ימות, ואל
תבעל לו. — תעמוד לפניו ערומה? — ימות ואל תעמוד
לפניו ערומה. — תספר עמו מאחורי הגדר? — ימות ולא
תספר עמו מאחורי הגדר. פליגי בה רבי יעקב בר אידי ורבי
שמואל בר נחמני. חד אמר: אשת איש היתה, וחד אמר:
פנויה היתה. בשלמא למאן דאמר אשת איש היתה —
שפיר. אלא למאן דאמר פנויה היתה מאי כולי האי? — רב
פפא אמר: משום פגם משפחה. רב אחא בריה דרב איקא
אמר: כדי שלא יהו בנות ישראל פרוצות בעריות. ולינסבה
מינסב! — לא מייתבה דעתיה, כדרבי יצחק, דאמר רבי
יצחק: מיום שחרב בית המקדש ניטלה טעם ביאה וניתנה
לעוברי עבירה, שנאמר (משלי ט׳) מים גנובים ימתקו ולחם
סתרים ינעם.

Rav Judah said in Rav's name, "A man once conceived a
passion for a certain woman, and his heart was consumed
by his burning desire for her. When the doctors were
consulted, they said, 'His only cure is that she shall submit
to him.' To which the Sages responded, 'Let him die
rather than that she should yield.' So the doctors said,
'Then let her stand nude before him.' The Sages answered,
'Sooner let him die.' 'Then,' said the doctors, 'let her
converse with him from behind a fence.' 'Let him die,' the
Sages replied, 'rather than she should converse with him
from behind a fence.'" Now Rabbi Jacob bar Idi and
Rabbi Samuel bar Nachmani have a dispute about this.
One said that she was a married woman, the other that she
was unmarried, due to the fact that this story makes sense

if she was a married woman, but if she was unmarried, why such severity? Rav Papa said, "Because of the disgrace to her family." Rav Acha the son of Rav Ika said, "So that the daughters of Israel may not be drawn into immorality." Then why did he not simply marry her? Because marriage would not assuage his passion, for as Rabbi Isaac has said, "Since the destruction of the Temple, sexual pleasure has been stolen from those who practice it lawfully and given instead to sinners, as it is written, STOLEN WATERS ARE SWEET, AND BREAD EATEN IN SECRET IS PLEASANT" (Proverbs 9:17).

What is meant by "stolen waters are sweet"?

Why do the Rabbis think that the man would not be romantically interested in the woman once they were married?

Do you think this would be true? Is a lessening of sexual or romantic interest inevitable after marriage? Why or why not? Can this be avoided? If so, how?

You may be surprised to find that even in talmudic times, contraception was an option.

Talmud, *Y'vamot* 35a

אשה מזנה משמשת במוך כדי שלא תתעבר.

A promiscuous woman makes use of an absorbent in order to prevent conception.

What questions does this text raise for you? What does this statement add to your understanding of the Rabbis' perspective on sex?

15. Sex Is Sacred

We have studied traditional Jewish texts together. Some are surprisingly liberal, while others are exceedingly restrictive. What they all share, however, is an overriding belief that sex, at least within the sanctity of marriage, is a sacred gift from God.

THE ZOHAR

The *Zohar*, or Book of Splendor, is the central work in the literature of the Kabbalah, or Jewish mysticism. It is believed that the main body of the *Zohar* was composed between 1270 and 1300 C.E., though it is attributed to Simeon bar Yochai, who lived in the second century C.E. Written in Aramaic, the *Zohar* reflects the teachings of the kabbalists, who sought to commune with God through the spiritual elevation of their souls.

Zohar, Section 2, Page 204b

אבל רזא דמלה דבר נש אית נפש דנטלא ומשיך לגביה
להאי רוחא מערב שבת. וההוא רוחא שריא בגווה דההיא
נפש ודיירא בה כל יומא דשבתא. וכדין ההוא נפש יתיר
ברבויא ותועלתא יתיר ממה דהוה. ועל דא תנינן כל נפשאן
דישראל מתעטרן ביומא דשבתא ועטרא דלהון דשרי׳ האי
רוחא בגוייהו. כיון דנפק שבתא וההוא רוחא סלקא לעילא
כדין ווי לנפש דאבדת מה דאבדת מה דאבדת. עונתן
דחכימין דידעי רזין עלאין מליליא דשבתא לליליא דשבתא
ואוקמוה.

But the truth is that man possesses a certain soul that attracts to itself the special spirit on the eve of Sabbath, so that that spirit takes up its abode and resides within it for the whole of the Sabbath. It thus becomes a superior soul, with greater power and resources than it possessed before. It is with regard to this that we have learned that the soul of every Israelite is adorned on the Sabbath day. This adornment consists of the additional Shabbat soul within them. At the conclusion of the Sabbath the special spirit departs, and then woe to the soul that is thus bereft. It has lost the heavenly crown and the holy energy it had possessed. And therefore those initiated in the higher wisdom perform their marital duties every Sabbath night.

According to the mystics we receive an additional soul on the Sabbath. Since sexual relations involve the mingling of souls as well as bodies, the *Zohar* here implies that sex on the Sabbath is a "double mitzvah." Those mystics "initiated in the higher wisdom" thus sought to have sexual relations with their wives specifically on the Sabbath.

Talmud, *Shabbat* 33a

אמר רבי חנן בר רבא: הכל יודעין כלה למה נכנסה לחופה,
אלא כל המנבל פיו אפילו חותמין עליו גזר דין של שבעים
שנה לטובה — הופכין עליו לרעה.

Said Rabbi Chanan bar Rabbah: All know for what purpose a bride enters the bridal canopy, yet if someone speaks obscenely of it, even if a decree of seventy years of happiness had been sealed for him, it is reversed in favor of misfortune.

How might someone speak obscenely about what happens on the wedding night?

What happens to one who does speak in such a way?

Why is this considered to be such a grave offense by the Talmud?

Talmud, *K'tubot* 17a

א"ר שמואל בר נחמני א"ר יונתן: מותר להסתכל בפני כלה
כל שבעה, כדי לחבבה על בעלה. ולית הלכתא כוותיה.

Rabbi Samuel bar Nachmani in the name of Rabbi Jonathan said, "It is permitted to look intently at the face of a bride throughout the seven days of celebration in order to make her more desirable to her husband." But the law is not according to him.

Why would Rabbi Samuel bar Nachmani permit what would normally be prohibited, to look lustfully at the bride of another man? What do you think of his advice? Would it work?

Why do you think the "law is not according to him"?

There is the sense in our tradition that marriages are "made in heaven." Consider this text from the midrash.

B'reishit Rabbah 68:4

רבי יהודה בר סימון פתח (תהלים סח) אלהים מושיב יחידים
ביתה מטרונה שאלה את ר' יוסי בר חלפתא אמרה לו
לכמה ימים ברא הקב"ה את עולמו אמר לה לששת ימים
כדכתיב (שמות כ) כי ששת ימים עשה ה' את השמים ואת
הארץ אמרה לו מה הוא עושה מאותה שעה ועד עכשיו
אמר לה הקב"ה יושב ומזווגים זיווגים בתו של פלוני לפלוני

אשתו של פלוני לפלוני ממונו של פלוני לפלוני אמרה לו
ודא הוא אומנתיה אף אני יכולה לעשות כן כמה עבדים
כמה שפחות יש לי לשעה קלה אני יכולה לזווגן אמר לה
אם קלה היא בעיניך קשה היא לפני הקב"ה כקריעת ים סוף
הלך לו ר' יוסי בר חלפתא מה עשתה נטלה אלף עבדים
ואלף שפחות והעמידה אותן שורות שורות אמרה פלן יסב
לפלונית ופלונית תיסב לפלוני וזיווגה אותן בלילה אחת
למחר אתון לגבה דין מוחיה פציעא דין עינו שמיטא דין
רגליה תבירא אמרה להון מה לכון דא אמרה לית אנא בעי
לדין ודין אמר לית אנא בעי לדא מיד שלחה והביאה את ר'
יוסי בר חלפתא אמרה לו לית אלוה כאלהכון אמת היא
תורתכון נאה ומשובחת יפה.

Rabbi Judah bar Simon began his sermon with the
biblical text, GOD CAUSES INDIVIDUALS TO LIVE IN THEIR
HOUSE (Psalm 68:7). A Roman matron asked Rav Yose bar
Chalafta, "In how many days did the Holy One, blessed
be, create the world?" "In six days," he answered. "Then
what has God been doing since then?" she mocked. "God
sits and makes matches," he answered, "assigning this
man to that woman, and this woman to that man." "If
that is what you call difficult," she gibed, "I too can do
the same." She then went and matched up her slaves,
giving this man to that woman, this woman to that man,
and so on. Before long, those who were thus united began
beating one another up, this woman saying, "I do not
want this man," and this man complaining, "I do not
want that woman." Immediately, she summoned Rav
Yose bar Chalafta and admitted to him, "There is no god
like your God. Your Torah is indeed beautiful and
praiseworthy, and you spoke the truth!"

Finally we find this beautiful text from the mystical tradition.

Zohar, Section 3, 59a

מכאן אוליפנא דבכל אתר דלא אשתכח דכר ונוקבא לאו
כדאי למחמי אפי שכינתא.

Where there is no union of male and female, people are not worthy to behold the Divine Presence.

16. Responsa Literature:
A Traditional Way of Dealing with Contemporary Issues

The process of Jewish legal development cannot be stagnant. Things change. New technologies are developed. Scientific breakthroughs alter our understanding of our world. History marches on. In order to respond to these changes, Judaism has developed responsa literature.

A new question arises. Local authorities are not confident what answer to give. The question is therefore sent to a trusted scholar for an opinion. This is called a שְׁאֵלָה (sh'eilah). The rabbi's response is called a תְּשׁוּבָה (t'shuvah), or responsum. Throughout the centuries such inquiries (sh'eilot) have been posed on every possible topic. The scope of the responsa literature, therefore, is vast. Together we will study only a few modern responsa (t'shuvot) to give us a feel for the nature of this genre. These t'shuvot will deal with difficult and controversial contemporary issues. Please understand, however, that a single responsum does not represent the Jewish answer to any given question. Jewish responses to these questions vary greatly from movement to movement, and often even within the various movements that make up the Jewish people.

Central Conference of American Rabbis

The CCAR, founded in 1889, is the rabbinic body representing Reform rabbis. This responsum is a product of the CCAR Responsa Committee and is published in *Teshuvot for the Nineties: Reform Judaism's Answers for Today's Dilemmas*, ed. W. Gunther Plaut and Mark Washofsky (New York: CCAR, 1999).

Teshuvot for the Nineties, Pages 171-176

Abortion to save siblings from suffering
5755.13

She'elah [Question]

I understand that abortion may sometimes be permissible under *Halachah* [Jewish law] if it is done to alleviate maternal suffering. Does this extend to relieve suffering of other family members that might be affected by this birth? For example, parents might choose to abort a handicapped fetus because they are concerned that it would impose an undue hardship on their other children who would be burdened by caring for this child in the future. The distinction is that the abortion would not be done to spare the mother suffering, but rather to spare the anguish of other family members. Would this be interpreted as a permissible reason for abortion?

Teshuvah [Answer]

The circumstances under which an abortion may be performed are the subject of intense debate within the halachic literature. The one basic principal upon which there is agreement—at least as a theoretical truth—is that fetal life has a lesser status than maternal life. This is evident from the Toraitic account [Exodus 21:22–23] of a fight between two men in which a pregnant woman is accidentally injured. If the fetus is lost but the woman survives, then the aggressor is punished with a fine, but if the woman is killed it is considered a capital crime, a case of *"nefesh tachat nefesh,"* demanding the life of the guilty party in recompense for the life lost.

This thinking is clearly reflected in the classic Mishnaic statement on abortion in Ohalot 7:6: "If a woman is in [life-threatening] difficulty giving birth, the one to be born is dismembered in her abdomen and then taken out limb by limb, for her life comes before its life. Once most of the child has emerged it is not to be touched, for one *nefesh* (person) is not to be put aside for another." Clearly, then, in cases where the mother's life hangs in the balance, the tradition supports abortion.

There is, however, a pivotal difference of opinion as regards the reasoning that leads to permission for abortion in such cases. Rashi [in a commentary to *Sanhedrin* 72b] states his conviction that—if the mother's life is threatened—so long as "the fetus has not emerged into the air of the world, it is not a *nefesh* and one is allowed to kill it in order to save its mother." Once it has emerged, it would become a case of *"nefesh tachat nefesh."* Rashi plainly bases his view, that it is permitted to kill the unborn fetus, on the grounds that the fetus—though alive—does not have the status of being a *nefesh*, and may, therefore, be sacrificed in the interests of saving the mother who is a fully developed *nefesh*.

Maimonides, however, while arriving at the same practical conclusion, does so via a very different route. [In his *Mishneh Torah* (*Hilchot Rotzeach* 1:9), Maimonides] takes up a theme—previously discounted by the rabbis in the Talmud—that the fetus who poses a threat to its mother's life should be seen as a *rodef*, as a pursuer coming to kill. The *halachah* encourages the killing of a *rodef* in order to prevent the *rodef* from killing. Maimonides puts it this way: "This, too, is a negative commandment: one must not take pity on the life of a *rodef*. Consequently, the sages taught: if a pregnant woman's labor becomes life threatening it is permitted to dismember the fetus in her abdomen, either by a medication or by hand, for it is like a *rodef* who is pursuing her to kill her...." Maimonides does not refer to any lesser status of the fetus; rather, he permits the killing of the fetus—so long as it has not yet emerged—because it is behaving like a *rodef* coming to kill its mother, and ought to be killed like any other *rodef*.

Maimonides, then, has been understood by numerous judges of the *halachah* to be of the view that in those instances where the fetus is not behaving like a *rodef*, no sanction exists to kill it. The prominent halachic strand which follows this outlook holds that the only acceptable circumstances for abortion are those in which the fetus poses a direct threat to the life of the mother. It should be noted that there are those within this school of thought who include the probability of insanity in the mother as a reason for abortion, since they regard insanity as a life-threatening condition. In the twentieth century, the halachic consensus, as represented by such figures as Chief Rabbi I. Y. Unterman and Rabbi Moshe Feinstein, continues to be characterized by this approach [Noam 6 (1963): 1–11; *Igerot Moshe*, Choshen Mishpat, vol. 2, no. 69].

It should be noted that unlike Rashi's interpretation—which closely tracks the plain sense of the Talmud—Maimonides' reasoning process, though popular, does not so readily conform to the thrust of the text. Later halachic literature clearly has to stretch in order to explain issues raised by Maimonides' *rodef* explanation....

While the majority of traditionalists nevertheless adhere to the Maimonidean interpretation, a minority does base its position on Rashi's logic. Since Rashi's approval for abortion—under conditions of a threat to the mother's life—is rooted in the inferior status of the fetus, it is possible to conceive of other menacing situations where the mother's superior interests might permit abortion. This is the line of reasoning used by those who take a more permissive approach to the question of acceptable criteria for abortion.

Explain the difference between the approach of Rashi and that of Maimonides with regard to the question of abortion.

How might their different perspectives affect the specific question at hand in this responsum?

Later in this CCAR responsum the authors deal more specifically with the issue of an abortion to spare a sibling emotional pain:

In only one or two *teshuvot* [responsa] have interests other than those of the mother been given any weight. A responsum by Rabbi Yitzchak Oelbaum from earlier this century presents an example. Rabbi Oelbaum was asked about a case in which a pregnant mother had an existent "weak" child who, according to the doctors, would not live unless it was breast-fed by its mother. The woman had noticed a change in her milk around the fourth week of pregnancy that seemed like it might be threatening to the nursing child. The mother wanted to know if she could abort the fetus in order to save the existent child. R. Oelbaum ... concluded that an abortion would be permitted if the experts were of the view that the existing child would indeed be in danger [*Sh'eilat Yitzchak* 64].

Oelbaum's judgment in this matter has, however, been the subject of great caution among most *poskim* [rabbinic authorities], who still view the halachic justification for abortion as extremis on the part of the mother [see M. Stern, *HeRefuah L'Or HaHalachah*, p. 104].

From the reasoning that has been put forward thus far, what answer do you believe the authors of this responsum will give to this question?

Now, let us see if you are correct.

Reform respondents have, historically, been aligned with those who are prepared to consider circumstances other than a threat to the mother's life as grounds for abortion. While tending towards a preference for lenient conditions, however, the thrust of the respondents' position has been succinctly summarized with the words "we do not encourage abortion, nor favor it for trivial reasons, or sanction it 'on demand'" [Walter Jacob, *Contemporary American Reform Responsa*, no. 16, p. 27]. Indeed, all the Reform responsa concerning this subject are careful to couch their lenient rulings within the general traditional understanding of the importance of alleviating "great pain" to the mother. None of them suggest that Judaism should countenance any other reason as a valid basis for abortion.

In the *she'elah* [question] that has been presented, the questioner definitively states that the proposed abortion "would not be to spare the mother suffering, but rather to spare the anguish of other family members." While Reform Judaism has, of course, forged new Jewish frontiers where compelling reasons deemed that a new path was the only "right and good" (*hayashar ve'hatov*) course to take, this case does not appear to warrant such action. Fetal life, though of lesser status than that of the mother, remains human life in potential, and is consequently of great significance. It can only be sacrificed for the most profound of reasons. Speculation and worry about the future are natural aspects of living, but do not themselves constitute a threat to the health of the mother sufficient to justify the termination of unborn life. Hence, Judaism could not give its assent to an abortion under these circumstances. If serious maternal anguish was the result of genuine fears over a defined handicap, then abortion could be contemplated, but certainly not for the sake of "hardship" or "quality of life" issues for other family members. It is the degree to which the mother is suffering "great pain" which remains determinative; the consideration of the anguish of others within the family is not pertinent to the question of an abortion.

What is your response to this responsum? Do you agree with its conclusion? Why or why not?

Not every responsum is accepted as governing principal by Judaism in general or even by the sponsoring Jewish movement. This relatively restrictive responsum, for instance, coexists with the many CCAR resolutions supporting a woman's right to choose abortion.[1] In our modern world, sometimes change is brought about by legislative democratic process, as in the case of the following CCAR resolution regarding single-sex marriage and commitment ceremonies. This resolution was passed overwhelmingly even though the CCAR Responsa Committee had previously issued a responsum discouraging such unions.[2]

Resolution on Same-Gender Officiation

Resolution Adopted at the 111th Convention of the Central Conference of American Rabbis March, 2000

Background

Over the years, the Central Conference of American Rabbis has adopted a number of positions on the rights of homosexuals, on homosexuality in the rabbinate, and advocating changes in civil law pertaining to same-gender relationships.

In 1977, the CCAR adopted a resolution calling for legislation decriminalizing homosexual acts between consenting adults, and calling for an end to discrimination against gays and lesbians. The resolution called on Reform Jewish organizations to develop programs to implement this stand.

In 1990, the CCAR endorsed the report of the Ad Hoc Committee on Homosexuality and the Rabbinate. This position paper urged that "all rabbis, regardless of sexual orientation, be accorded the opportunity to fulfill the sacred vocation that they have chosen." The committee endorsed the view that "all Jews are religiously equal regardless of their sexual orientation." The committee expressed its agreement with changes in the admissions policies of the Hebrew Union College–Jewish Institute of Religion, which stated that the "sexual orientation of an applicant [be considered] only within the context of a candidate's overall suitability for the rabbinate," and reaffirmed that all rabbinic graduates of the HUC–JIR would be admitted into CCAR membership upon application. The report described differing views within the committee as to the nature of *kiddushin*, and deferred the matter of rabbinic officiation.

A 1996 resolution resolved that the CCAR "support the right of gay and lesbian couples to share fully and equally in the rights of civil marriage," and voiced opposition to governmental efforts to ban gay and lesbian marriages.

In addition to these resolutions, two CCAR committees have addressed the question of same-gender officiation. The CCAR Committee on Responsa addressed the question of whether homosexual relationships can qualify as *kiddushin* (which it defined as "Jewish marriage"). By a committee majority of 7 to 2, the committee concluded that "homosexual relationships, however exclusive and committed they may be, do not fit within this legal category; they cannot be called *kiddushin*. We do not understand Jewish marriage apart from the concept of *kiddushin*." The committee acknowledged its lack of consensus on this question.

The Ad Hoc Committee on Human Sexuality issued a report in 1998 which included its conclusion, by a committee majority of 11 with 1 abstention, that "*kedushah* may be present in committed same-gender relationships between two Jews and that these relationships can serve as the foundation of stable Jewish families, thus adding strength to the Jewish community." The report called upon the CCAR to support all colleagues in their choices in this matter, and to develop educational programs.

RESOLUTION

WHEREAS justice and human dignity are cherished Jewish values, and...

WHEREAS, the institutions of Reform Judaism have a long history of support for civil and equal rights for gays and lesbians, and

WHEREAS, North American organizations of the Reform Movement have passed resolutions in support of civil marriage for gays and lesbians, therefore

WE DO HEREBY RESOLVE, that the relationship of a Jewish, same-gender couple is worthy of affirmation through appropriate Jewish ritual, and

FURTHER RESOLVED, that we recognize the diversity of opinions within our ranks on this issue. We support the decision of those who choose to officiate at rituals of union for same-gender couples, and we support the decision of those who do not, and

FURTHER RESOLVED, that we call upon the CCAR to support all colleagues in their choices in this matter, and

FURTHER RESOLVED, that we also call upon the CCAR to develop both educational and liturgical resources in this area.

Please articulate five arguments against the passage of this resolution.

Now articulate five arguments in favor of the passage of this resolution.

If you were asked to vote on this resolution, how would you vote? Why?

No contemporary sexual issue is more difficult to articulate than is the question of premarital sex. In his "'This Is My Beloved, This Is My Friend': A Rabbinic Letter on Intimate Relations" (pp. 30–35), Rabbi Elliot N. Dorff tackles this thorny issue with great tact and perspicacity. While not a product of the Rabbinical Assembly's Responsa Committee per se, his paper, excerpted here, is in the spirit of the age-old question-and-answer process that makes up the vast and ever-growing legal tradition known as the responsa literature.

The Rabbinical Assembly

The Rabbinical Assembly, founded in 1901, is the international association of Conservative rabbis. This paper was published by the Commission on Human Sexuality of the Rabbinical Assembly (New York, 1996). Please keep in mind that, since it was published in 1996, some of the technical medical details may be slightly out of date.

"'This Is My Beloved, This Is My Friend': A Rabbinic Letter on Intimate Relations"

Non-Marital Sex

Judaism posits marriage as the appropriate context for sexual intercourse. We recognize, though, that many Jews are engaging in sexual relations outside the marital bond. Some of these sexual acts are adulterous, incestuous, or involuntary, and we resoundingly condemn them as a gross violation of Jewish law. . . . We also condemn casual and promiscuous sexual encounters since they involve little or no love or commitment.

The non-marital relations which this section addresses, then, are not adulterous, incestuous, forced, or promiscuous; they are rather sexual relations between two unmarried adults which take place in the context of an ongoing, loving relationship. People engage in such relations for a number of reasons: because a suitable mate has not yet been, or may never be, found, often despite painful and heartfelt searching; because one's life circumstances render marital commitment premature, often for emotional, educational, economic, or professional reasons; or because experience with divorce or the death of a partner has necessitated a gradual healing process, including experience of several transitional relationships prior to remarriage.

We want to say at the outset of this section that it is perfectly natural and healthy for unmarried people to hug and kiss each other as signs of friendship and warmth.... Romantic relationships, from their earliest stages and throughout their unfolding, often use these forms of affection too. Holding hands, hugging, and kissing are perfectly natural and healthy expressions of both a budding romance and a long-term one. One must take due regard for the sense of modesty and privacy which Judaism would have us preserve in expressing our romantic feelings, and so the more intense forms of these activities should be reserved for private quarters. Within those norms, though, unmarried as well as married people routinely do and should engage in these practices as they build and strengthen the loving relationships which make them distinctly human.

The remainder of this section, then, deals exclusively with the issue of sexual intercourse outside of marriage.... Only marriages can attain the holiness and communal sanction of *kiddushin* [holiness] because it is the marital context which holds out the most promise that people can live by those views and values in their intimate relationships. Judaism would therefore have us refrain from sexual intercourse outside marriage.

Why does Judaism posit marriage as the appropriate context for sexual intercourse? It does so because in that setting the couple can attain the three-fold purposes for marital sex described above—namely, companionship, procreation, and the education of the next generation. While non-marital sex can provide companionship as well as physical release, especially in the context of a long-term relationship, unmarried couples generally do not want to undertake the responsibilities of having and educating children. They may care deeply for each other, especially in a long-term relationship, but their unwillingness to get married usually signifies that they are not ready to make a life-long commitment to each other.

Some people, though, either will not or cannot get married, and the physical and psychological pleasures which sex provides lead them to engage in sexual relations with each other. Judaism cannot condone such relationships. Nevertheless, for those Jews who do engage in them, all of the concepts and values described . . . above apply to their sexual activities. That is, Jewish norms in sexual matters, like Jewish norms in other arenas, are not an "all or nothing" thing. Certainly, failing to abide by Judaism's command that we restrict sexual relations to marriage does not excuse one from trying to live by the concepts and values Judaism would have us use in all of our relationships, including our intimate ones. In fact, in the context of non-marital relationships, some of them take on new significance:

1. *Seeing oneself and one's partner as the creatures of God.* We are not machines; we are integrated wholes created by, and in the image of God. As such, our sexual activity must reflect our value system and the personhood of the other. If it is only for physical release, it degrades us terribly. While this recognition is a necessary component in marital sex, it is all the more imperative in non-marital sex, where the lack of a public, long-term commitment to one another heightens the chances that one or both of the partners will see sex as simply pleasurable release. In our sexual activities, we need to retain our human character— indeed, our divine imprint.

2. *Respect for others.* This means, minimally, that we must avoid coercive sex. Marriage is no guarantee that sexual relations will be respectful and non-coercive. Still, the deep relationship which marriage betokens makes it more probable that the two partners will care for each other in their sexual relations as well as in all of the other arenas of life. Unmarried people must take special care to do this, if only because they know each other less well and are therefore more likely to misunderstand each other's cues.

3. *Modesty.* The demand that one be modest in one's sexual activities—as well as in one's speech and dress—is another corollary of seeing oneself in the image of God. For singles it is especially important to note that modesty requires that one's sexual activities be conducted in private and that they not be discussed with others.

4. *Honesty*. Marriage is a public statement of commitment of the partners to each other, and sexual activity is one powerful way in which that commitment is restated and reconfirmed. If one is not married, however, sex cannot possibly symbolize the same degree of commitment. Unmarried sexual partners must therefore openly and honestly confront what their sexual activity means for the length and depth of their relationship.

5. *Fidelity*. Marriage by its very nature demands fidelity; unmarried relationships by their very nature do not. The value of fidelity, then, and the security, intensity, and intimacy that it imparts to a relationship are not really available to a non-marital relationship. In the spirit of this value, though, one should avoid short-term sexual encounters and seek, instead, a long-term relationship to which one remains faithful for the duration of the relationship. Infidelity breeds pain, distrust, and, in the extreme, inability to form intimate relationships with anyone. The Jewish tradition requires us to respect one another more than that; we minimally must be honest and faithful to our commitments so as to avoid harming one another.

6. *Health and safety*. This concern of the Jewish tradition is even more critical in non-marital relationships than it is in married ones, for most sexually transmitted diseases are contracted in non-marital, sexual liaisons. In our time, this includes not only recurring infections, like syphilis, but fatal diseases like AIDS.

From the standpoint of Judaism, marriage is the appropriate place for sexual relations. For those not living up to that standard it is imperative to recognize that sexual contact with any new partner raises the possible risk of AIDS. That is not only a pragmatic word to the wise; it comes out of the depths of the Jewish moral and legal tradition, where *pikuah nefesh* (saving a life) is a value of the highest order. Moreover we are commanded by our tradition to take measures to prevent illness in the first place. Fulfilling these commandments in this age requires all of the following:

(a) full disclosure of each partner's sexual history from 1980 to the present to identify whether a previous partner may have been infected with the HIV virus;
(b) HIV testing for both partners before genital sex is considered, recognizing all the while that a negative test result is only valid six months after the last genital contact;
(c) careful and consistent use of condoms until the risk of infection has been definitively ruled out either by the partner's sexual history or results of HIV testing; and
(d) abstinence from coitus where there is demonstrated HIV infection in either partner.

If any of these requirements cannot be met, due to discomfort with open communication, lack of maturity, one partner's reticence to disclose his or her history, or doubts about the trustworthiness of the partner's assurances, then abstinence from genital sex with this partner is the only safe and Jewishly legitimate choice. AIDS, after all, is lethal; protection against it must be part of any sexual decision. We are always obligated to take care of our bodies, and that responsibility does not stop at the bedroom door. Sexual relationships must therefore be conducted with safety concerns clearly in our minds and hearts.

7. *The possibility of a child.* Unmarried couples should recognize that, even with the use of contraceptives, an unplanned pregnancy is always a possibility. Abortion may not be used as a retroactive form of birth control: Jewish law forbids abortion for non-therapeutic reasons. From the perspective of Jewish law, the fetus is not a full-fledged human being, but as a part of its mother and as a potential human being, it may not be aborted except when the life or physical or mental health of the mother requires it. "Mental health" here, as noted earlier, does not include simply not wanting to have a child. Consequently, couples engaged in non-marital sexual relations must use contraceptives, and they must be prepared to undertake the responsibilities of raising a child or giving it up for adoption if one results. All of the couple's options—raising the child, abortion, and even giving up the baby for adoption, the choice that may seem the least onerous—involve serious psychological consequences for all concerned, and, in the case of abortion, moral and sometimes physical ones as well. The implications of a possible pregnancy must therefore be carefully considered.

8. *The Jewish quality of the relationship.* Unmarried people who live together should discuss the Jewish character of their relationship just as much as newlyweds need to do. That ranges across the gamut of ritual commandments, such as the dietary laws and Sabbath and Festival observance, and it also involves all of the theological and moral issues described above.

Moreover, single Jews should date Jews exclusively so as not to incur the problems of intermarriage for themselves and for the Jewish people as a whole. Intermarriage is a major problem for the contemporary Jewish community, for studies indicate that some 90% of the children of intermarried couples are not raised as Jews. Furthermore, intermarriage is a problem for the people themselves. Marriage is hard enough as it is, involving, as it does, many adjustments of the couple to each other; it is even harder if they come from different religious backgrounds. It is no wonder, then, that as high as the divorce rate is among couples of the same religion, it is almost double that among couples consisting of a Jew and a non-Jew. Consequently, single Jews should date Jews exclusively if they want to enhance their chances of staying together and of having Jewish children and grandchildren.

It should be clear from this discussion of the Jewish values relevant to sex that it is very difficult to live by them in the context of unmarried relationships. That, in fact, is a major reason why Judaism understands marriage to be the proper venue for sexual intercourse in the first place. We affirm the correctness and wisdom of that stance.

Nevertheless, committed, loving relationships between mature people who strive to conduct their sexual lives according to the concepts and values described above can embody a measure of morality, although not the full portion available in marriage. Indeed, serious Jews who find themselves in transitional times of their lives should feel duty-bound to invest their relationships with these concepts and values. Only then can their Jewish commitment have some of the meaning it should for the sexual components of their lives. That meaning can flourish all the more when and if they find themselves ready and able to marry, but Judaism should affect their sexual activities before and after then as well.

What is your reaction to Rabbi Dorff's perspective on premarital sex?

In what ways do you agree with him?

In what ways do you disagree with him? Why?

In your mind's eye, try to age yourself fifteen years. How will you feel about his advice then? Will your perspective have changed? Why and how?

17. Conclusion

I warned you! Jewish texts are anything but consistent in their attitudes toward human sexuality. Together, we have studied texts that are prudish and conservative, as well as some that sound as if they could have been written by Dr. Ruth.

Amidst all of this cacophony, however, have you been able to discern any consistent trends, recurring themes, or reliable tendencies in our tradition? If so, what are they?

What appeals to you the most about Jewish perspectives on sex? Why?

What disturbs you the most? Why?

What do you want to know more about?

Afterword

Now that you have shared your reactions, let me share mine with you.

In my study of these Jewish sources, I have found that Jewish texts are often more human and forgiving than we would expect.

I have found that Jewish sources, although often sexist, are also marked by an abiding appreciation for, and sense of wonder at, the innate goodness and holiness of women.

I have found that Jewish attitudes towards sexuality have changed throughout time and vary from community to community. This is most apparent in the Jewish view of homosexuality. What is clear is that regard for the dignity of the individual is great in our tradition, even if we disagree about the various behaviors of those individuals.

I have found that, in Judaism, sex is not bad, or evil, or dirty. To the contrary, Jewish sources often idealize sexuality. Not only is sexual pleasure within a committed marital relationship acceptable, it is holy.

Now our study is at an end. Together we have shared the sacred process of exploring Jewish texts together. Thank you for joining me in this endeavor. The study of Jewish texts, however, is a lifelong quest. Go and study!

Notes

[1] The following resolution, for instance, was adopted by the CCAR at its 91st Annual Convention in Pittsburgh, Pennsylvania, June 23–26, 1980:

In 1967 the Conference stated: "We strongly urge the broad liberalization of abortion laws in various states, and call upon our members to work toward this end."

The Conference reaffirms this position with the following comments:

A. Jewish legal literature permits therapeutic abortion.

B. The decision concerning any abortion must be made by the woman and not by the state or any other external agency.

C. We oppose all constitutional amendments and legislation which would abridge or circumscribe this right.

D. We call upon our rabbis and upon the Union of American Hebrew Congregations to strengthen their support of the Religious Coalition for Abortion Rights on national, state, and local levels.

[2] See Jacob, Walter, ed. *Contemporary American Reform Responsa*. NY: CCAR Press, 1987, pp. 297–298. See also CCAR Responsa Committee #5756.8.

Printed in the USA
CPSIA information can be obtained
at www.ICGtesting.com
JSHW011729090424
60867JS00004B/179